EMPIRES ASCENDANT

TimeFrame 400 BC–AD 200

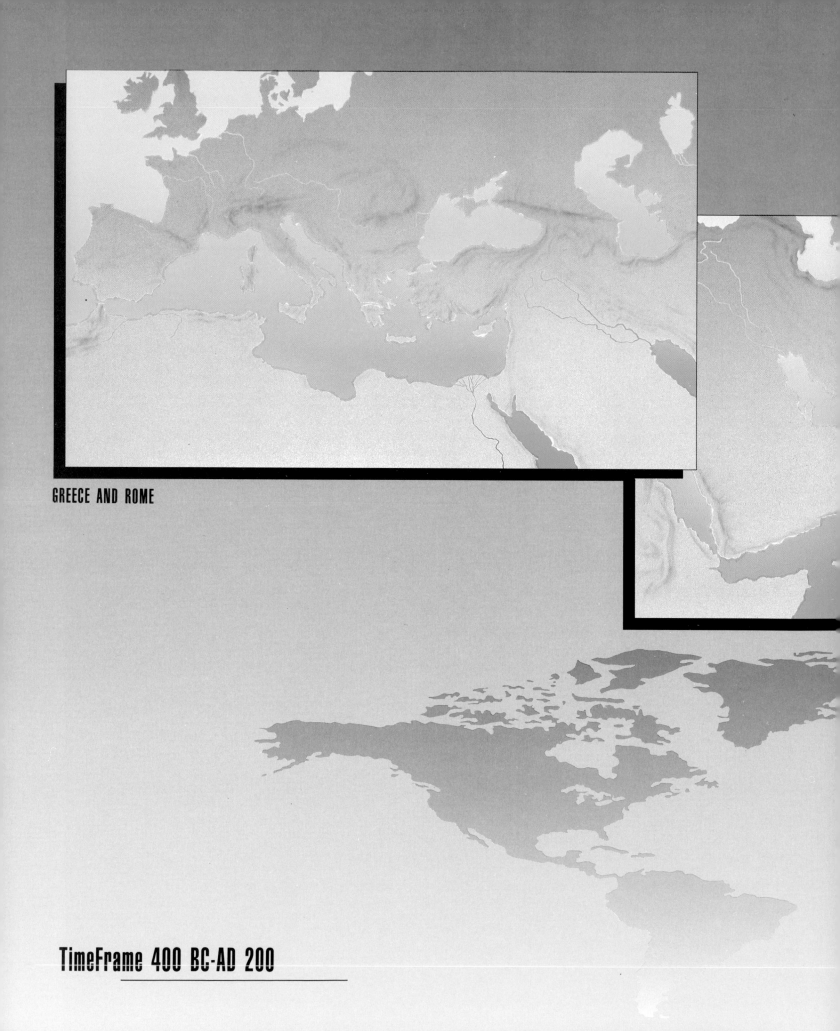

GREECE AND ROME

TimeFrame 400 BC-AD 200

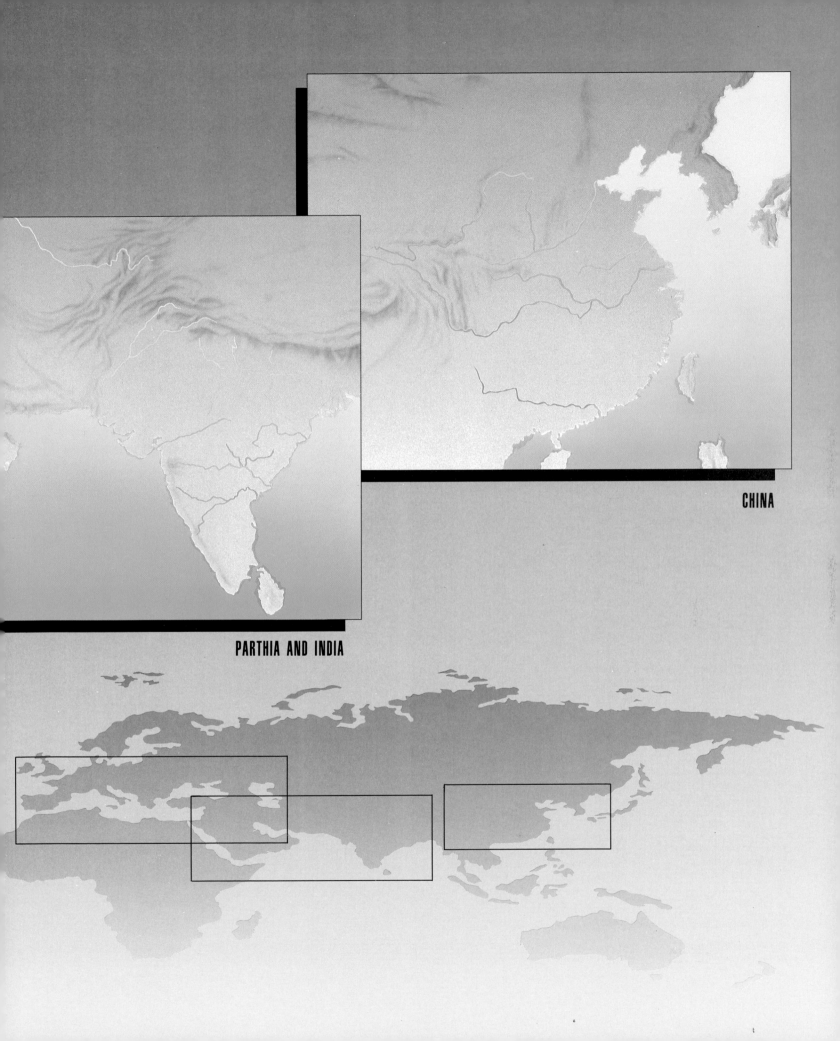

CHINA

PARTHIA AND INDIA

EMPIRES ASCENDANT

TimeFrame 400 BC–AD 200

BY THE EDITORS OF TIME-LIFE BOOKS

TIME-LIFE BOOKS, ALEXANDRIA, VIRGINIA

Time-Life Books Inc.
is a wholly owned subsidiary of
TIME INCORPORATED

FOUNDER: Henry R. Luce 1898-1967

Editor-in-Chief: Jason McManus
Chairman and Chief Executive Officer:
J. Richard Munro
President and Chief Operating Officer:
N. J. Nicholas, Jr.
Editorial Director: Ray Cave
Executive Vice President, Books:
Kelso F. Sutton
Vice President, Books: George Artandi

TIME-LIFE BOOKS INC.

EDITOR: George Constable
Executive Editor: Ellen Phillips
Director of Design: Louis Klein
Director of Editorial Resources:
Phyllis K. Wise
Editorial Board: Russell B. Adams, Jr.,
Dale M. Brown, Roberta Conlan, Thomas
H. Flaherty, Lee Hassig, Donia Ann Steele,
Rosalind Stubenberg, Kit van Tulleken,
Henry Woodhead
Director of Photography and Research:
John Conrad Weiser

PRESIDENT: Christopher T. Linen
Chief Operating Officer: John M. Fahey, Jr.
Senior Vice President: James L. Mercer
Vice Presidents: Stephen L. Bair,
Ralph J. Cuomo, Neal Goff, Stephen
L. Goldstein, Juanita T. James, Hallett
Johnson III, Carol Kaplan, Susan
J. Maruyama, Robert H. Smith, Paul
R. Stewart, Joseph J. Ward
Director of Production Services:
Robert J. Passantino

Editorial Operations
Copy Chief: Diane Ullius
Production: Celia Beattie
Quality Control: James J. Cox (director)
Library: Louise D. Forstall

Correspondents: Elisabeth Kraemer-Singh
(Bonn); Maria Vincenza Aloisi (Paris); Ann
Natanson (Rome). Valuable assistance
was also provided by: Mirka Gondicas
(Athens); Philip Cunningham, Jaime
A. Florcruz, Jane Zhang (Beijing);
Dean Fischer (Cairo); Caroline Alcock,
Christine Hinze, Caroline Lucas, Linda
Proud (London); Arti Ahluwalia (New Del-
hi); Elizabeth Brown, Christina Lieberman
(New York); Josephine du Brusle (Paris);
Ann Wise (Rome); Dick Berry (Tokyo);
Traudl Lessing (Vienna).

TIME FRAME

SERIES DIRECTOR: Henry Woodhead
Series Administrator:
Philip Brandt George

Editorial Staff for *Empires Ascendant:*
Designer: Tom Huestis
Associate Editors: Jim Hicks (text); Marion
F. Briggs (pictures)
Writers: Stephen G. Hyslop, Brian
Pohanka
Researchers: Karin Kinney (text); Jane
A. Martin, Paula York-Soderlund (pictures)
Assistant Designers: Elissa Baldwin,
Barbara McClenahan
Copy Coordinators: Vivian Noble, Jarelle
S. Stein
Picture Coordinator: Renée DeSandies
Editorial Assistants: Lona Tavernise,
Patricia D. Whiteford

Special Contributors: Ronald H. Bailey,
Champ Clark, George G. Daniels, Donald
Dale Jackson, Brian McGinn, David S.
Thomson, Bryce Walker (text); Mariana
Tait Durban, Ann-Louise G. Gates, Brian
Miller, Barbara Moir, Robbie D. Steel
(research); Roy Nanovic (index)

CONSULTANTS

China:
JACK L. DULL, Associate Professor, Department of History, University of Washington, Seattle, Washington

SUN JI, Museum of People's History, Beijing

Greece and Rome:
JOSIAH OBER, Professor, Department of
History, University of Montana, Bozeman,
Montana

MARY T. BOATWRIGHT, Associate Professor, Department of Classical Studies,
Duke University, Durham, North Carolina

MAX KUNZE, Direktor, Antikensammlung, Staatliche Museen zu Berlin, East
Berlin

India:
VIMALA BEGLEY, Research Associate,
University of Pennsylvania Museum, Iowa
City, Iowa

Military History:
JOHN FRANCIS GUILMARTIN, JR., Asso-
ciate Professor, Department of History,
Ohio State University, Columbus, Ohio

**Library of Congress Cataloging in
Publication Data**

Empires ascendant.
  Bibliography: p.
  Includes index.
  1. History, Ancient. I. Time-Life Books.
D57.E47 1988   930   87-18054
ISBN 0-8094-6412-8
ISBN 0-8094-6413-6 (lib. bdg.)

Time-Life Books Inc. offers a wide range of fine
recordings, including a *Rock 'n' Roll Era* series.
For subscription information, call 1-800-621-
7026 or write Time-Life Music, P.O. Box C-
32068, Richmond, Virginia 23261-2068.

CONTENTS

THE ODYSSEY OF ALEXANDER THE GREAT

All through the hot summer of 321 BC the glittering procession inched along, like some great golden caterpillar, slowly traveling westward from Babylon. At each city along the route, from every hinterland village, crowds gathered to stare in awe, to offer their homage and lamentations. Never had there been such a magnificent display: the golden carriage with its garlanded columns and gem-encrusted vault, a miniature Greek temple on wheels; the elegant train of sixty-four high-stepping mules, yoked four abreast, collars studded with jewels, gold bells on their halters chiming as they walked; the joined regiments from Persia and Macedonia marching in solemn grief and honor; and beneath the temple portico, canopied in purple, fragrant with spices, the coffin of hammered gold. For the emperor was dead, Alexander the Great, conqueror of Egypt and Asia, supreme lord and hero to half the known world, cut down by fever at the age of thirty-three. And now his body was being carried home from Babylon for burial.

But where was home? Alexander had been born in Macedonia, a primitive Greek state northwest of the Aegean, but had not set foot there in more than a decade, ever since embarking on a sweeping campaign of conquest. In that time he had founded scores of cities, naming sixteen of them after himself. He had taken one wife in Persia and another in Afghanistan, after bending both lands to his will. Egypt worshiped him as a god. His upbringing had been Greek, and he saw Athens as the hub of world culture — although he thought it sadly degraded in other ways. The final seat of his empire was Babylon, where his body had lain in state for the twenty-four months it had taken to prepare his catafalque. What place could properly claim him, then, this man who lived where he found himself, at the constant center of his own imperial glory? More than any other individual of his day, Alexander was a citizen of the world.

The practical issue of where his body would end up was decided by one of Alexander's generals. Ptolemy, a boyhood friend who ruled as satrap of Egypt, marched an army to Syria, and there awaited the cortege with the stated intent of doing it homage. The procession was headed for Macedonia. But Ptolemy seized control and turned the gleaming carriage and golden coffin toward Egypt.

A tomb of dazzling splendor soon took shape at Alexandria, the splendid city the emperor had raised on the Nile Delta, and there his body would remain for centuries, attended by priests and worshiped by pilgrims. Julius Caesar paid his respects in 48 BC, as did Caesar's successor, the emperor Augustus, who like many other Romans wore Alexander's visage on a cameo ring. Early Christians would depict Jesus in the conqueror's image, clean-shaven and with flowing blond hair. Centuries later, the Moslems would enroll him as a saint. "It is a lovely thing to live with courage, and to die leaving an everlasting fame," Alexander once remarked.

Any warrior of Alexander's time would have understood this thirst for glory and

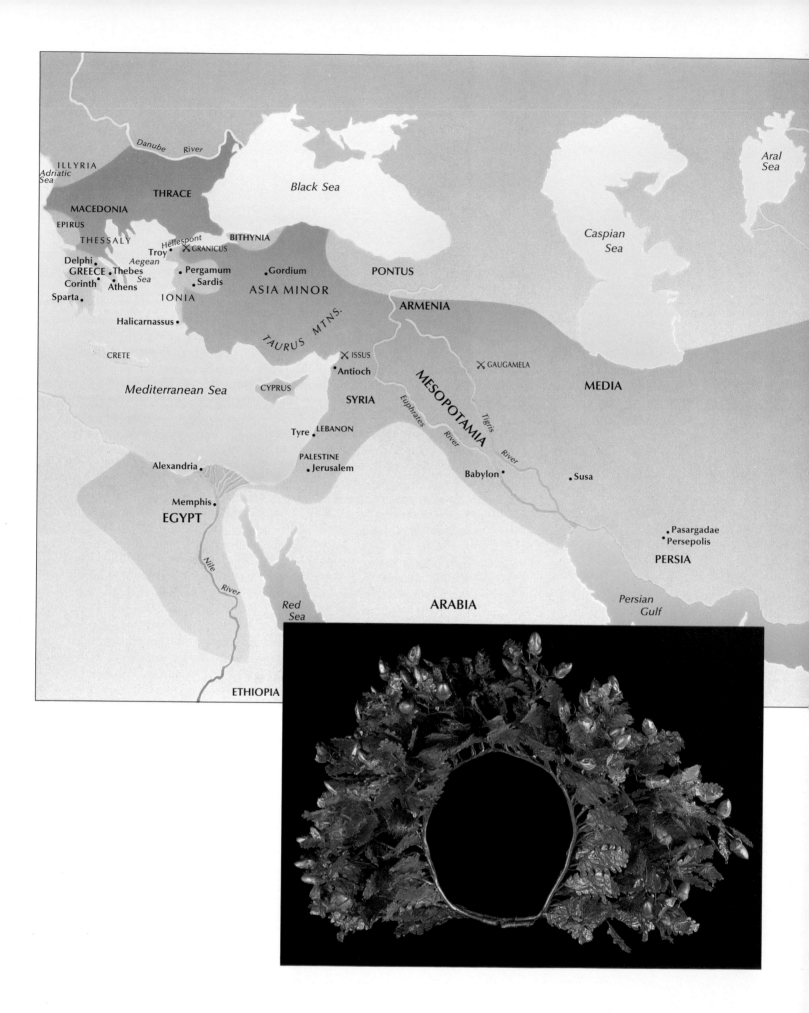

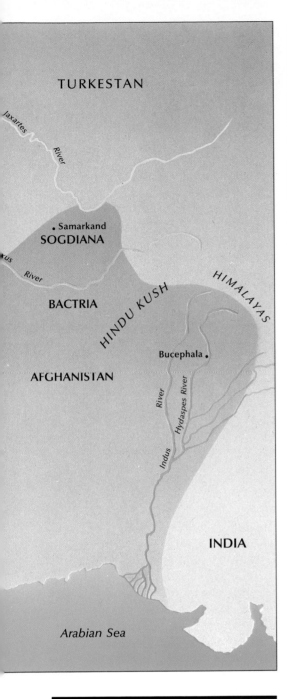

TURKESTAN

Jaxartes River

• Samarkand
SOGDIANA

us River

BACTRIA

HINDU KUSH

HIMALAYAS

Bucephala •

AFGHANISTAN

River

Hydaspes River

Indus River

INDIA

Arabian Sea

In a mere eleven years of campaigning, Alexander the Great amassed the most extensive empire the world had ever seen. It sprawled over parts of three continents, from Alexander's native Macedonia in Europe into northern Africa and across western Asia to India. In his conquests, the youthful monarch vanquished Persian armies in major battles (crossed swords) at Granicus, Issus, and Gaugamela, and brought the old Persian empire under his rule. Alexander was inspired by the warlike example of his father, Philip II, whose treasures included a glorious wreath of golden oak leaves (inset).

adventure; it was as basic to the mental climate of the fourth century BC as the verses of Homer. But Alexander's vision extended far beyond the common experience of his day, and particularly that of his fellow Greeks. Heretofore in the Aegean world, loyalties had focused largely on tribal leaders or on feudal lords or cities. The rulers of the immense Persian empire had successfully engaged the loyalties of diverse peoples far and wide. But the Greeks, in their victorious campaigns, had made little attempt to enlist the fealty of the vanquished. Even so renowned a sage as Aristotle — who had been Alexander's childhood tutor — tended to regard anyone not born a Greek with a certain sad contempt, as being of a lesser race.

The youthful Alexander, scarcely in his twenties when he first ascended the throne of Macedonia, clearly saw the futility in that. His father, Philip II, a powerful and cunning king, had struggled mightily to unite the fractious Greeks. And the son firmly grasped the ideal. Alexander strove to weld the nations under his imperial scepter into a single entity, while allowing them to maintain their own religious and cultural institutions. Slaughter, pillage, slavery, so brutally familiar in the ancient world, held little attraction for Alexander; although he was a fearsome commander, an appeal to reason and trust, a sharing of goals were for him the ultimate tools of power. It is true that his empire did not long survive him: It splintered into scores of smaller nations. Yet the Greek language and culture that Alexander had transported throughout the lands he conquered remained as a residue of unity, held in common among the fragmented and rival states. This legacy of Alexander's endured for centuries.

But far more than that, the Alexandrian model of empire found new expression in later centuries. The vision of a unified world came to life in the Rome of the first century BC. The imperial ideal, rooted in conquest but flourishing with peace and enlightenment, swept irresistibly through India and was powerfully ascendant among the Parthians on the dusty Iranian plateau. Entirely coincidentally, a parallel vision gathered force in far-off China at this same time, leading to a sophisticated empire that eventually ordered the lives of some sixty million people.

The rise of these great political and cultural entities all the way across the vast Eurasian landmass, from western Europe to the Far East, resulted in a momentous development, one that was more significant than the fact of their individual existences or the advance in government organization that they represented. Through trade and diplomacy and war, the new empires reached out and discovered one another. For the first time, the ancient civilizations of West and East and regions in between began to learn what a large and varied world they occupied, and to establish ties through which ideas as well as merchandise were exchanged.

The states around the Aegean entered the fourth century — some fifty years before Alexander's birth — in disarray from the Peloponnesian War. That conflict had set Greek against Greek, scourged cities, toppled governments, and temporarily devastated economic life. When the war finally ended in 404 BC, the victor — if it could be called that — was Sparta. The city's arch-rival Athens, once dominant in Greece, had been reduced to hapless submission — its walls torn down, its colonies stripped away, its once-mighty navy rotting on the sea floor. But Spartan hegemony was brief and bloody. Ruled by a narrow and overbearing class of military oligarchs, Sparta wielded its power with a disastrously rigid hand. It invaded a neighboring city-state, Elis, and virtually destroyed it. It annexed nearly all of Athens's overseas possessions, installing its own garrisons and puppet oligarchs. And it embarked on what proved to be an imprudent expedition to liberate the Greek city-states of Ionia from rule by Persians.

While Spartan forces were fighting in Asia Minor, a number of Sparta's neighbors banded together and prepared for war. Corinth, Thebes, Argos, Athens — none was particularly potent by itself, but as a group they were strong enough to confront Sparta. The Corinthian War opened in the spring of 395 BC and continued, off and on, for nearly a decade, in the course of which Athens emerged once again as a power. By 380 BC the city's walls were rebuilt and the navy revived. A new Athenian League took shape, drawn up along more equitable lines than before, as a confederacy rather than a collection of vassal states.

Another city-state to reassert its influence was Thebes. The Thebans rebuilt their army and threw off the Spartan yoke. The army's new strength derived, in part, from an elite infantry corps, the Sacred Band, composed of 150 pairs of highborn youths who had sworn blood brotherhood and who were trained to a keen fighting edge. The Thebans also invented a new kind of battle formation in which a phalanx was deepened and strengthened in one section by the addition of many extra ranks of soldiers. And they employed a new tactic: charging at an oblique angle instead of head-on, so that the weighted section of the phalanx could pierce an opposing line like a battering ram. Their new techniques proved their worth in 371 BC, when the ever-aggressive Spartans launched a full-scale attack on Thebes and were swiftly put to rout.

Over the next decade, Theban power grew rapidly, and now the other Greek states, which at first had seen Thebes as a champion of liberty, took alarm and gathered their forces. Alliances fractured, partners switched sides, new wars raged from one end of Greece to the other. Athens, campaigning on several fronts, met with reversals; its alliance began breaking up. The Thebans were again victorious over Sparta in 362 BC, but before long returned to their wheat farms and cow pastures. New peace treaties were signed. But nothing had been settled; exhaustion alone had ended the hostilities.

A profound change of attitude set in during these decades, a basic shift in people's values and perceptions. The first signs of change had appeared at Athens — always in the intellectual vanguard — as early as the Peloponnesian War. The city had suffered terrible hardship and had seen a generation of its bravest men perish on the battlefield. In an earlier time, the highest glory had been to sacrifice life and fortune for the good of the city. But now public service increasingly gave way to self-interest. In some cases this was unavoidable. Soldiers returned from the battlefields to find their farms overgrown and untillable. They had to keep soldiering in order to support their families. If their own cities happened temporarily to be at peace, they would hire out as mercenaries in the armies of other states. In the past, each citizen had been expected to shoulder the burden of his own city's defense; now the task more often than not passed to these paid professionals. At the same time, the old ideal of the universal man, proficient in trade or farming, fighting, politics, sports, and the arts, began to give way to a new recognition that excellence came with specialization. Professional athletes competed at the Olympian games, and professional musicians filled the orchestras at theatrical festivals, where before amateurs had played for the love of the art.

These changes increased tensions between the wealthy and the class of small landowners and free peasants, who once were the heart of Athenian society. As economic disruption widened the gap between rich and poor, each group became suspicious and wary of the other. Civic morality went into decline; lawsuits increased dramatically, and bribery and blackmail became more common.

Yet even as the old values diminished, the foundations for a new intellectual life were being laid. Exciting new inspiration appeared in the arts. Idealized portraits of gods and heroes started giving way to realistic images of ordinary men. Certain early dramatists had foreshadowed this trend, and their work grew in popularity: Euripides, with his probing of the human psyche; and Aristophanes, with his unflattering portrayals of contemporary figures. A similar naturalism swept painting and sculpture. Such artists as Praxiteles and Scopas paid great attention to the features of individuals and to the nuances of passing emotion. Realism was all. Of a painting by one of the new Greek artists, the playwright Herodas wrote: "That naked boy: If I scratched him, wouldn't it leave a mark? For he has flesh on him that quivers with life on the panel."

The young art of history took on a previously unknown immediacy, becoming a sort of prejournalism exemplified by the work of Xenophon, an Athenian who in 401 BC joined a group of Greek mercenaries that went to fight in a Persian civil war. In gripping detail, Xenophon chronicled the adventures of the 10,000 Greeks, the valiant battles, the fighting retreat, and the Greek escape to the sea.

"Man is the measure of all things," the Sophist philosopher Protagoras had written in the late fifth century BC, referring to humankind as a whole. To the Greeks of the fourth century, a key issue was the character of the individual. And the swing to personal concerns gained strong — though unintended — impetus from the teachings of Athens's most illustrious sages. But in 399 BC, an event occurred that seemed certain to stifle free expression. The philosopher Socrates, among many things a forceful critic of Athenian-style democracy, was formally accused of corrupting the minds of the city's youth.

The charges were perhaps understandable. Athenian democracy had just been restored after a period of oppressive tyranny — and the worst of the tyrants had been one of Socrates' own pupils. In court to defend himself, the sage ridiculed the charges rather than addressing them. "I am a sort of gadfly, given to the state by God," he declared. He refused to go along with a plot by his friends to spirit him into safe exile, choosing instead to drink the state's deadly draft of poison hemlock.

Nothing drives home a person's ideals more powerfully than self-martyrdom, but Socrates' teachings would have lived on in any case. Discarding all preconceived standards of thought and behavior, equating virtue with truth, he subjected everything around him to relentless questioning. "An unexamined life is not worth living," he observed. He argued that the highest moral standards were not those of society but those set by each individual's conscience. The idea was revolutionary.

Indeed, one group of Socratic disciples, led by Diogenes of Sinope, rejected the very notion of the city-state and claimed allegiance to the world at large, as brothers of all humanity. To free themselves from society's constraints they reduced their lives to the utmost simplicity. Happiness, they believed, could be found only in a return to primitive self-sufficiency, unencumbered by duties or possessions. Diogenes reportedly showed the way by abandoning home and family and taking up residence in a large barrel. To other Greeks, it all seemed so cheerless that Diogenes and his followers were said to "live like dogs"; they became Cynics, from the Greek word for "canine."

Another disciple, Aristippus of Cyrene, also forswore the state but otherwise took an opposite view, maintaining that happiness lies not with deprivation but, most obviously, with gratification. Thus was born hedonism, the pursuit of *hēdonē* — pleasure. But at first, at least, it did not mean a total surrender to orgiastic appetites; discrimination was essential, and true hedonists learned to master their desires.

The most renowned of Socrates' pupils was Plato, an Athenian whose voluminous

Cornered by a lion while hunting in the game preserve of the king of Sidon, Alexander *(below, left)* is rescued by his faithful officer Craterus in this mosaic from the town of Pella in Macedonia. In killing a lion, Alexander was attempting to emulate the mythical hero Herakles, with whom he claimed kinship and in whose guise — crowned with a lion skin — he was sometimes represented *(inset)*.

writings rank among the most profound philosophical documents of any age. Political-ly active as a young man, Plato was horror-stricken by his mentor's death, and he quit public life to reflect, write, and travel abroad. Returning to Athens in 387 BC, he founded a school, the Academy, where he employed the endlessly questioning Socrat-ic method to open the minds of a new generation of wealthy Greek youth.

What Plato taught was formidable. Going beyond Socrates, he ventured into a realm of almost mystical abstraction. Appearances were deceptive, the senses useless in determining truth. For behind the objective, everyday world of tables, houses, horses, and mountaintops, there lay a region of abstract forms, or ideas. Here was the natural habitat of all things true and beautiful, the wellspring of creativity, and the final resting place of the human soul. The universe as it is perceived by the senses is a crude

approximation, a pale shadow cast by the divine flame, which is nothing less than thought itself.

Ambitious young Athenians and other Greeks gravitated to Plato's Academy, where they hoped to acquire mental strength and agility — some in hopes of playing a leading role in civic affairs, others simply in quest of the truth. Although Plato had retired from public life, politics continued to fascinate him. Like Socrates, he distrusted Athenian democ-racy, which he considered weak and ineffectual. But even though de-mocracy was imperfect, clearly there had to be a government; otherwise, all would be chaos. In *The Republic,* he proposed his ideal version of a city-state — authoritarian and supremely stable, with a classless citizenry ruled by benevolent philosopher-kings.

Among Plato's students was a youth from Macedonia, Aristotle of Sta-gira, who arrived in Athens at the age of seventeen to attend the Acade-my. Although Plato and Aristotle shared many concerns, their minds worked in different ways. Plato was intuitive and poetic; Aristotle viewed the world through the cool, objective eyes of the laboratory scientist. Aristotle's chief interests were biology and medicine, but he took all knowledge as his preserve, and he was constantly noting down details of weather, metaphysics, political science, and human behavior — all ar-ranged into systematic categories. Sometimes Aristotle's ardent empiri-cism led to absurdities. As a definition of "man," for example, he fixed upon "a warm-blooded creature that walks on two hind legs." When someone pointed out that the same definition could be applied to a chicken, Aristotle revised it to read, "a warm-blooded creature with five toes and no feathers. . . ."

Nowhere were the differences between Aristotle and his teacher so clearly drawn as in their political theories. Whereas Plato began with a concept for an ideal state, then filled in its details of law and administra-tion, Aristotle set out by compiling data. He made a minute study of 150 Greek regimes, comparing their laws and weighing one against the other. He was more sympathetic than Plato to democracy, but in the end Aristot-le's ideal state was similar to that outlined in Plato's *Republic.*

The search for better government preoccupied a number of other con-temporary thinkers. One advocate of basic reform was Isocrates, a fa-mous teacher of rhetoric and an intellectual rival of Plato. The conten-tious Greek states must cease quarreling, he declared, and unite their interests in a confederacy. Only then would social unrest decline and stability return. The idea of cooperation between states had been gaining currency among the war-weary Greeks for some time, but no one pursued it as energetically as Isocrates. He knew that only a powerful leader could bring about such cooperation.

No such paragon had yet been discovered, despite much searching by Isocrates and others. But the leader was there, gathering his strength in the backward, mountainous kingdom of Macedonia. He was the young Philip II — determined, crafty, unscrupulous, brilliant, perhaps not the morally superior man Isocrates had in mind, but strong enough to do the job.

Few Greeks gave much thought to Macedonia. The region was so primitive that it seemed to belong to another age — it was a rude, brawling, heavy-drinking country of dour peasants and landowning warriors who would have fit comfortably in the pages of Homer. The language was Greek, but so tainted by barbarian strains that Athenians could not understand it. The current ruling house claimed descent from Herakles and made an effort to smooth the kingdom's roughhewn nature with a veneer of Greek culture; the court at Pella became a center of imported Hellenic art and literature. Yet Macedonia remained an outland, and succession to the throne tended to occur by dagger or spear, as in some ancient tragedy retold by Aeschylus.

Philip's ascent was in keeping. Appointed regent at the age of twenty-three for his infant nephew — his brother, the king, had died in battle — Philip bought off or otherwise eliminated three half brothers to retain his position. At the same time he defeated two foreign invasions. Somehow in all the scuffling, the infant heir vanished, and in 359 BC Philip persuaded the army to declare him king.

Once power was his, the young monarch swiftly brought order to his domain. By armed force when necessary, by diplomatic guile whenever he could, he spread his control north into Thrace, west toward Epirus, and south into Thessaly. Macedonia lacked access to the sea; Philip captured the coastal Athenian colony of Amphipolis, then cleverly duped the Athenians into giving him Pydna as well. The Macedonian state treasury was meager; he filled it by taking the Thracian mines at Mount Pangaeus, which produced 1,000 gold talents a year.

Wherever he gained territory, Philip founded cities, built roads, promoted farming, and strove to win the loyalty of his new subjects. Those who resisted met with force, yet the king always preferred to achieve his objectives without shedding blood. "The credit for a military victory," he would say, "I share with my soldiers; for a diplomatic victory, it is all mine."

The true instrument of Philip's success was nonetheless his superb standing army. The Macedonian force was made up of career professionals, and no one was more of a soldier than the king himself. Some years before, when Macedonia had had a new peace treaty with Thebes, the teenage Philip had been sent to live there as guarantee of good faith. Thebes was at the height of its power and boasted the strongest military establishment in Greece. Philip studied the army's structure and training, the role of the elite Sacred Band infantry unit, and the quick-strike tactics of the phalanxes. Applying these lessons to his own troops, he created the most disciplined fighting force in the Aegean. His own phalanxes, marshaled in the deep Theban fashion,

Alexander's powerful warhorse Bucephalus, in this sculpture girded with a chest strap bearing the fearsome image of Medusa, carried his master safely through dozens of campaigns and battles. The high-strung steed would allow no one else to ride him, yet in Alexander's presence became docile enough to kneel so that the king could easily step into the saddle. When the horse died in India from the effects of old age and wounds, Alexander founded a city named Bucephalia in his honor.

were armed for tremendous striking power with spears of great length — including, eventually, the mighty *sarissa,* a fifteen-foot weapon that may have been of Philip's own devising. When these ranks lowered their spears and rushed forward in unison, it was as if a wave of death-dealing steel had swept over the enemy. The phalanxes typically struck at the heart of the enemy line, while fast-moving cavalry, wielding short javelins, ripped away at the flanks.

Philip himself invariably led the charge — and his body carried the evidence. In one campaign, an arrow pierced his right eye. In another, his shoulder was smashed; in yet another, a lance thrust so mangled his thigh that he nearly died. He walked with a limp ever afterwards. Yet neither pain nor fear seemed to touch him.

He backed up his conquests by clever diplomatic marriages and by building a cohort of devoted warriors. He acquired seven wives — most to seal political alliances, but some for affection's sake. Physical love between men was an accepted reality of the Hellenic world, and in warrior society, the ideal of heroic manhood carried strong romantic overtones. Such in fact was the organizing principle of the Theban Sacred Band, on the theory that pairs of warrior-lovers would defend each other to the death. Although contemporary observers did not record whether Philip had male lovers, he did surround himself with a cadre of handsome young nobles, the Companions, who fought alongside him in battle and advised him in peace.

As Philip's battlefield exploits mounted, his Hellenic neighbors grew anxious about the rising Macedonian colossus. And for good reason: War had broken out again in central Greece, setting Athens against Thessaly and Thebes and involving several other states. Philip had been awaiting just such an opportunity. He moved his army into Thessaly on the pretext of defending it, and for good measure scooped up a number of Athenian possessions to the north. Bribery, charm, bullying, force — any method served to extend his power. Informed that the walls of a particular city were impregnable, he responded: "So impregnable that even gold can't scale them?"

Philip grew ever stronger while the war between Athens and the other states continued. And when at last, in 346 BC, the exhausted combatants were ready to sign a peace, Philip was in a position to dictate its terms. In the process, he named himself defender of the shrine of Apollo at Delphi, which entitled him to preside over the athletic games held there in that same year. It was a role of immense prestige. The onetime petty prince of a barbarian state was now the most important man in Greece.

And so the long-sought hero had appeared. Isocrates, now in his nineties, wrote a long letter urging Philip to assume command of a united Greece, and to lead its armies into Asia. The expedition would be a crusade to free the captive Ionian cities from their Persian overlords, and to seize Persian wealth in vengeance for the destruction the Persians had wreaked in Greece more than a century earlier. Both ideas were enormously popular among the Greeks.

Some Greeks mistrusted Philip, however, and they found a spokesman in the brilliant orator Demosthenes. Demosthenes had commenced his career under a severe handicap, a speech impediment that legend said he overcame by practicing speaking with pebbles in his mouth. His orations rang with power and logic. And he clearly saw the future under Philip: If this domineering Macedonian won control of Greece, it would mean the end of the democratic city-state and the death knell of liberty for every Greek. He stated this view in many speeches, including the three brilliant *Philippics,* masterpieces of thundering denunciation.

As Demosthenes predicted, so it came to pass. Philip used an incident at Delphi as an excuse to invade central Greece. The combined armies of Thebes and Athens met his phalanxes in 338 BC at Chaeronea, and they crumpled under the onslaught. Philip's son, the young prince Alexander, then eighteen years old and in command of the left-wing cavalry, was ranged against the hitherto invincible Sacred Band. Encircled by Macedonian horsemen, the Band held out, refusing to surrender, until every last soldier perished.

Philip cremated the battlefield dead. He placed a garrison in Thebes, but he took no reprisals. Athens he simply left alone, releasing his Athenian prisoners. He did not even march to the city to accept a victor's traditional homage. Perhaps he did not wish to embarrass the Athenians, whom he admired and whose support he wanted. Skirting the city, he marched south to the Peloponnesus, securing it without a struggle.

Then Philip called an assembly of states at Corinth, where he announced the rules by which Greece would be governed. Henceforth, no Greek would make war against another Greek, but all would unite for the common good. The states would retain their autonomy in local government. They would pay Philip no tax or tribute, other than to supply men or ships to a federated Greek force, commanded by him. However, the ultimate authority was his alone, and if any city stepped out of line, it would have to answer to him. Philip then reiterated Isocrates' proposal for a crusade into Asia to rescue the captive Ionian cities and defeat the Persians.

The great crusade would take place — but not in Philip's time. For while success followed success in Greece, his control of the Macedonian heartland had begun to weaken. Enemies in his court focused much of their plotting on his own queen, Olympias, the mother of Alexander. Olympias was the sister of the king of Epirus, and Philip had married her in part for political reasons. They may also once have loved each other, but by the time Alexander was an adolescent, Olympias's main concern was less for her husband than that her son should succeed him. The uneasy relationship continued for some years. The king's five other wives were, like Olympias, foreign born; but they were docile and posed no threat to her premier position. However, in 337 BC — when Philip was forty-eight and, ventured the historian Plutarch, "past the age for such things" — he entered into a love match with a Macedonian maiden of noble blood. Olympias was infuriated. Her prestige was in jeopardy, and a Macedonian woman might bear a son who could displace her own Alexander as heir apparent.

According to Plutarch — who did not shrink from employing dialogue in his biography of Alexander, although he wrote it about four centuries after the events described — Olympias remained in her quarters, fuming, during the marriage feast. But Alexander attended, and as the wine flowed, his own temper grew short. The bride's uncle, in a toast, managed to insult the young prince, and in response Alexander hurled a drinking cup at him. Philip lurched up from his couch to restore order. But the king's head was spinning with wine, and his crippled leg gave way. "Look at him," taunted Alexander. "He is planning to cross from Europe to Asia, but he cannot cross from one couch to another without stumbling." Then the prince stalked from the hall. Mother and son retired to Olympias's ancestral home in Epirus. Eventually Alexander was persuaded to return to the palace, but his mother stayed behind.

The next year Philip held another royal wedding, this one calculated to repair his domestic relations. One of his daughters was marrying Olympias's brother, the king of Epirus. It was a celebration in grand Hellenic style, with parades, feasting, and a festival of the arts. Then, disaster. As Philip entered the stadium to preside, a bodyguard named Pausanias stepped forward and ran a sword through the king's heart.

Many people assumed that the assassin must be in the pay of Olympias. Others were of the opinion that he had been bribed by the Persians. And some people suggested that Pausanias might have had reasons of his own for murdering Philip. One story said that he had been viciously raped by a gang of courtiers — perhaps by way of retribution for some earlier offense of his — and that he was enraged when Philip refused to punish his assailants. In any case, the king was dead. Long live the king.

If any man was born to conquer, it was Alexander. Son of a great soldier, he had been nurtured on tales of heroism and high adventure. At an early age, he could quote from memory Homer, Euripides, and Pindar; in the palace or on campaign, he slept with the *Iliad* near his pillow.

He seemed the incarnation of ancient ideals and was extravagantly proud. Asked as a child if he wanted to compete in the Olympian games, Alexander replied, "only if I have kings to run against me." Yet he treated his men as equals. Once in power, he advanced his subordinates on ability rather than on birth. Impulsive and outgoing, with a need for friendship that was almost religious in its intensity, he tied people to him with bonds of loyalty and affection. On the eve of a battle he would stroll among his men, chatting with them about past exploits. Afterward he would visit the wounded.

Part of Alexander's appeal was sheer physical presence. Though not a large man, he radiated energy and strength. His body had been hardened by his continuous training; he once refused a queen's offer of her best chefs, declaring that

Some of the contingents in Alexander's army can be identified in this spirited frieze from a Phoenician tomb, showing the conqueror's troops locked in battle with Darius's Persians. Those labeled Companions, both cavalry and infantry, were members of an elite band of young nobles. Although Macedonians formed the core of Alexander's force, its ranks included detachments from most of the Greek city-states, as well as allied contingents from the kingdoms of Asia Minor. This heterogeneous force was welded together by the common bonds of discipline, training, and organization, as well as the devotion that Alexander inspired.

Many of Alexander's soldiers wore the so-called Phrygian helmet *(above)*. The bronze headgear was commonly painted blue, and helmets worn by officers were decorated with feather crests or plumes.

SENIOR SOLDIER OF FOOT COMPANIONS   COMPANION CAVALRYMAN

the best cook of all had been his first schoolmaster, who had regularly treated him to "a night march to make me want breakfast, and a small breakfast to make me want dinner." And then there was that magnetic visage, as depicted on coins, statues, paintings, and mosaics for centuries: the fair skin, the tousled blond hair and clean-shaven chin, the curiously innocent eyes that gazed at the world with "a certain melting look," as Plutarch described it. When Alexander entered a room, he both seduced and mastered it.

Two incidents illustrated his brilliance. In the first, a fine stallion was presented for sale to Philip, but the beast appeared to be so wild that no one could handle it. Alexander, then scarcely in his teens, asked to try, and declared that he would forfeit the asking price if he failed. The adults all chuckled. But the sharp-eyed youngster had noticed something no one else had: The horse was shying at its own shadow. He calmly turned the stallion's head to the sun, quieting it, then mounted and cantered off. Thus did Alexander win Bucephalus, his mount in battle for years afterward.

"My boy," declared Philip, "you must find a kingdom big enough for your ambitions. Macedonia is too small for you." The real point was not so much ambition but wits and audacity — an unequaled ability to grasp a situation and act on it.

The second incident occurred some years later on campaign in Asia Minor. In the town of Gordium, a chariot was rigged to its shaft with a knot so intricate that no one could untangle it; by local myth, the person who succeeded in doing so would come to be lord of Asia. Alexander studied the knot a moment, then simply pulled out a pin that the knot was tied around, collapsing it. He had seen a direct solution and applied it. In another version of the tale, he cut the Gordian knot with his sword.

The devils of self-doubt apparently never plagued Alexander. He had an utter confidence, astonishing in one so intelligent and thoroughly schooled. His principal tutor, Aristotle, had been brought by Philip from Athens. The philosopher had drilled his royal pupil in science and medicine, in government and literature. During his march through Asia, Alexander sent back botanical specimens for Aristotle's perusal; and on campaign he surrounded himself with geographers, astronomers, geologists, meteorologists, and artists, as if he were exploring instead of making war.

But the essential lesson of Greek learning, from Socrates on down, was to question everything, and this lesson Alexander missed. His purpose clear, he never questioned.

And the young king's one purpose was conquest, starting where his father had left off. Among the books popular in Greece during Alexander's youth were the histories of

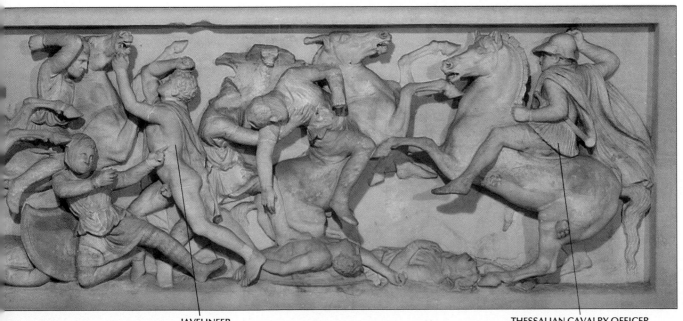

JAVELINEER   THESSALIAN CAVALRY OFFICER

Herodotus, with their saga of a Greece united against the Persian invader, and Xenophon's account of the Ten Thousand. Two of Philip's generals had already established a bridgehead across the Hellespont, in Asia Minor. The cruel but capable Persian ruler Artaxerxes Ochus had been poisoned by his own grand vizier, and the untried Darius III held the imperial scepter. Surely now was the time to launch the Asian crusade.

Yet Alexander was only twenty and appeared somewhat vulnerable himself. No sooner had he ascended the throne than the fabric of conquests and alliances woven by his father showed signs of unraveling. Revolt flared in Thrace, and Alexander

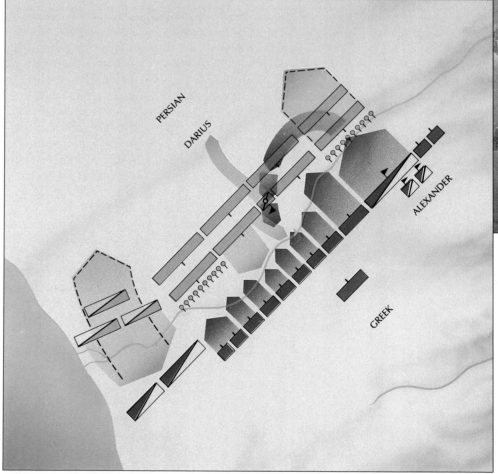

Alexander, without a helmet, gallops in pursuit of King Darius's chariot in this mosaic illustrating the climax of the battle of Issus. The hard-fought engagement was a striking example of Alexander's mastery of tactics and his ability to triumph in the face of odds that were seemingly insurmountable. Despite the fact that Darius's troops occupied a formidable defensive position behind the Pinarus River, and the Greek forces were outnumbered ten to one, Alexander took the offensive. While the Macedonian infantry pinned down the Persian center, Alexander himself led a cavalry charge against the enemy's left wing (to the right on the map). Riding through a hail of arrows, the Macedonian horsemen splashed across the Pinarus River, plowed through the Persians, wheeled left, and began rolling up Darius's battle lines. Although there was fierce resistance on the part of the Persian Royal Guard and a large detachment of Greek mercenaries, Darius's forces fragmented and fled. Alexander did not capture Darius, but that evening he dined amid the splendors of the Persian's treasure-laden royal pavilion.

marched north to quell it, then led his phalanxes against the wild tribes of Illyria, extending Macedonia's holdings north to the Danube and west to the Adriatic. Meanwhile, however, rumors spread that Alexander had been slain in battle. Several members of Philip's Corinthian League, led by Thebes, rose in rebellion.

Alexander turned and charged into Greece, quick-marching the 300 miles from Illyria to Thebes in just twelve days. He stood before the city's gates and demanded its surrender. When the Thebans refused, his soldiers stormed the walls and the streets, killing, burning, pillaging, raping. Six thousand Thebans were slaughtered; another 20,000 were sold into slavery. So terrible was the destruction that Alexander, troubled with regrets for once in his life, made a pilgrimage to Delphi as an act of contrition. But thereafter no Greek city openly defied the young king.

Alexander then visited Corinth to revive the League and enlist support for his Asian crusade. Among the city's residents was the Cynic philosopher Diogenes, and as Corinth's notables filed past to pay their respects, Alexander kept hoping to see the great savant among them. When he failed to appear, the king went in search of him. Alexander found him sprawled stark naked, taking a sunbath. "Is there any assistance we may bring you?" Alexander respectfully inquired.

"Yes," answered Diogenes. "You may stand a little to one side, out of my sun." This impertinence sent a ripple of muttering through the king's aides. Alexander quickly silenced them. "Were I not Alexander," he declared, "I would be Diogenes."

Alexander commenced his Asian adventure in the spring of 334 BC, marching out from Pella through fields of crimson poppies and yellow mustard with 30,000 foot soldiers and 5,000 cavalry. It was a tiny force with which to assail a continent, but its leader put his faith in speed and daring. At the Hellespont, Alexander left the crossing to his generals while he steered a galley for Troy, there to lay a wreath on Achilles' grave. He also came away with an ancient Homeric shield, which he would bear into battle as a talisman of heroic prowess.

The first real battle, against an equal Persian force at the river Granicus, was won by the momentum of a cavalry charge. The young commander rode at the head, galloping across the spring torrent and scrambling up the slippery bank, the double plumes on his helmet streaming out conspicuously like twin white banners. In the hand-to-hand melee that ensued, an enemy spear clanged against Alexander's breastplate, and a battle-ax split his helmet, but neither penetrated his skin. Terrified by the sheer fury of the Macedonians, the Persians turned and fled.

In the next weeks Alexander marched down the Ionian coast as the liberator Greece had prayed for. City after city threw open its gates. At Sardis, he restored the city's ancient laws and built a temple to Zeus. In Caria, the queen adopted him as an honorary son. Several cities, heavily garrisoned by Persian troops, required force. Miletus, a major Persian naval base, was Alexander's after a surprise assault; a brief siege brought the surrender of Halicarnassus, another important Persian port.

By now Ionia had been largely cleared of Persian forces. The crusade might reasonably be deemed a success, and the army returned home. But two objectives had to be met before Alexander could regard his victories as permanent. The Persian navy, a major instrument of imperial power, had to be immobilized, and a crippling defeat had to be delivered to the main Persian army.

Alexander pushed east through Asia Minor, down through the Tarsus Mountains via a narrow pass — its defenders fled at the news of his approach — and out onto the Mediterranean coastal plain above Syria. The Persian Darius, now fully alert to the threat from the west, had mobilized an army to confront it. Along the shore at Issus the two forces met: 35,000 Macedonians against a host of perhaps 300,000 men, including a number of Greek mercenaries, led by Darius himself.

If the first Asian battle had been won through speed and boldness, Issus was a triumph of tactics. The Persians anchored their defense between the mountains and the sea, a cramped position that allowed no room for their superior numbers to maneuver. Alexander deployed his troops to maximum effect, flanks covered by his lightning-fast cavalry, his center secured by the strong Macedonian phalanxes. As the sides engaged, he saw a weak spot in the enemy line and lanced through it.

Darius observed the battle from the rear in an ornate chariot. He watched in horror as his line wavered, fell back, and then disintegrated. Through the dust of battle, he spied Alexander astride Bucephalus; the Macedonian warrior-king galloped straight for him. Darius's nerve broke, and he fled the field.

Scarcely stopping to count his spoils, Alexander marched south down the coast,

TEMPLES OF HEALING

Although Hellenic peoples everywhere believed that a number of their gods possessed miraculous curative powers, one deity in particular, Asklepios by name, was especially venerated as the divine physician, god of medicine, and patron of the sick. People who were afflicted with chronic illnesses or the infirmities of age often sought sanctuary in the temples of this benevolent god, for *Asklepieia* were not only places of worship but places of healing.

Some temple buildings were used for bathing and ritual exercise, and others served as sleeping pavilions, since Asklepios was said to practice his healing in the hours of darkness. As part of the medical treatment, patients often handled dogs and snakes, both of which were sacred to the god. But complex surgical procedures, such as some types of eye operations, were also employed, and temple physicians were credited with a high rate of cure.

A temple physician massages a patient's shoulder *(left),* while a priestess, serving as a nurse, looks on. Although medical treatment at *Asklepieia* was free, a recovered patient was expected to make a votive offering, which sometimes took the form of a replica of the afflicted organ or limb *(above).*

capturing one Persian stronghold after another. Tyre, massively fortified on an island just off shore, seemed impregnable and temporarily slowed his advance. He had to construct a causeway out from land, then roll in siege towers. It took seven months to subdue Tyre, and Alexander subjected its citizens to an unusually harsh fate, sending 30,000 of them into slavery. He may have wished to eliminate any chance of future trouble. Or he may have been infuriated that the defenders had violated the traditional sanctity of messengers by murdering the men he sent with an ultimatum.

Tyre was an exception. Like Philip before him, Alexander preferred to be generous in victory. His troops were forbidden to pillage, and reprisals were seldom made. He won the goodwill of natives by sending quartermasters ahead with money to buy large supplies of food for his soldiers. The young conqueror tried his utmost to respect local customs, to revere local gods, to administer captured lands through existing hierarchies, and to win the populace to his side.

Moving south, he swiftly marched through Palestine and across the desert to Egypt, the last of Persia's Mediterranean holdings. He strode to the Nile as though leading a triumphal parade. The Egyptians, chafing under Persian rule, welcomed him as a liberating messiah. In Memphis, the capital, he offered sacrifices to the Egyptian gods. Then he journeyed 300 miles to the desert shrine of Ammon, whom the Greeks equated with Zeus. Alexander hoped to pay tribute to the god, but the high priest greeted him as though he were a god himself: "Hail, son of Ammon." Soon it was being said that the conqueror's true father was not Ammon — nor Philip — but the last Egyptian pharaoh, who supposedly had visited Alexander's mother in Macedonia disguised as a soothsayer. In any event, Alexander, like the pharaohs before him, was worshiped by the Egyptians as a deity.

Yet the conqueror's most permanent legacy on the Nile was not a matter of religion, or even of government. It was a city, the second of his sixteen Alexandrias. (The first, in Syria, commemorated his victory at Issus.) Legend said that he chose the site from a description in Homer, then laid out its walls with barley meal from the soldiers' mess.

Strategically placed on the Nile Delta, Alexandria rapidly grew into the handsomest, most cosmopolitan seaport on the Mediterranean, with a fine double harbor and a 440-foot lighthouse, the Pharos, that was regarded as one of the wonders of the world. And future generations of scholars would flock to Alexandria's great library.

Alexander did not linger in Egypt, however. His march of conquest had assumed a momentum of its own, and he turned to the north, then resumed his eastward thrust, following the arc of the fertile crescent into Mesopotamia. Some months earlier, Darius had sent an envoy to sue for peace, offering his daughter in marriage, 10,000 gold talents, and one-third of his empire. "If I were Alexander, I would accept," advised the top-ranking Macedonian general, Parmenion. "So would I, were I Parmenion," Alexander replied. For the commander's horizons had broadened greatly since crossing the Hellespont. The fantastic vistas of new lands and new cultures and the thrill of conquest had inspired in him dreams far greater than Philip had ever imagined. Alexander now demanded nothing less than the entire Persian empire.

The Persian king again mobilized an enormous army and prepared to meet the invader at a point east of the Tigris. Darius chose the battlefield with great care: a plain at Gaugamela, with enough open ground to give full scope to his greater numbers; he further improved the field by plowing it table-flat. He must surely avoid the cramped position that had spelled disaster at Issus. And he also wanted to make ample use of a fearsome weapon — fifty chariots with scythe blades attached to their wheels, designed to scatter an enemy phalanx.

Alexander arrived at the hills overlooking Gaugamela in late afternoon and watched as the plain began to sparkle with the light of enemy watchfires. His generals urged a surprise night attack, since the Macedonian army was outnumbered by perhaps five to one. Alexander refused. "I will not steal my victory," he said, and with an air of supreme confidence retired to his tent. For he had a plan, based on the superior speed and discipline of his own troops and the special temperament of his adversary Darius.

Next morning as the battle opened, Alexander trotted his cavalry obliquely to the right in a maneuver designed to throw the enemy line off balance. Darius fell for the ruse and ordered his troops to follow — soon to find many of them stumbling about in the rough terrain beyond his carefully prepared field. In the center, meanwhile, the Persian commander drove his scythed chariots at the advancing Macedonian phalanxes. "Rolling forward like a flood," as Plutarch described it, the Macedonians suddenly opened ranks so that the chariots rushed harmlessly through to the rear, where waiting cavalry dealt with them. Scarcely a Macedonian was killed or injured.

Alexander now saw the opportunity he knew must come. There was a momentary thinning of the Persian line, and he started through it, personally leading the charge and making straight for Darius's chariot. As at Issus, Darius turned tail and fled.

Utterly humiliated, the Persian monarch retreated to Media, his empire slipping away like sand through his fingers. Alexander progressed easily from one Persian territorial capital to the next, meeting only scattered resistance. Babylon threw open its golden gates and staged a month-long festival in honor of its new overlord. Susa readily capitulated. Near Persepolis, the local satrap attempted to hold his ground but was quickly overrun. It was a costly move; Alexander repaid him by allowing the victorious troops a rare bout of pillaging.

In capturing Persepolis, Alexander acquired the main treasury of the Persian empire, an immense hoard of gold and such a wealth of gems, silks, artifacts, and furnishings that 2,000 pairs of mules and 500 camels were required to remove it. He also gained the empire's spiritual heart, the ceremonial seat where vassal lords assembled each year to pay tribute to the King of Kings. A short march across the Iranian plateau brought him to Pasargadae, where Cyrus the Great, the imperial founder, lay buried. Cyrus had long been one of Alexander's idols — brave in war, magnanimous in victory, and a wise and tolerant ruler. The young Macedonian entered the great man's tomb and remained there some hours alone, quietly meditating. Then he ordered some needed repairs and renovations and returned to Persepolis.

Alexander remained some months in Persepolis, resting his troops. He hunted, played a kind of volleyball, dispensed favors, and attended to state business — its volume having grown steadily in proportion to his conquests. Then an appalling event took place. During a feast, drunken revelers tossed lighted torches into Persepolis's

Fixed forever in rhythmic motion, a Grecian terra-cotta couple (opposite) step out in a gavottelike dance while a graceful female companion swirls to an unheard melody. Both music and dance, considered by the Greeks to be among the highest forms of art, were usually present in rituals and theatrical performances. Because women were often excluded from these formal activities, they did their dancing on more mundane occasions, such as wedding feasts. Many courtesans, or hetairai, were accomplished musicians, skilled in playing stringed instruments — such as the lyre and kithara — that provided the accompaniment to the various forms of dance (above).

MENANDER'S NEW COMEDY

The most successful Greek dramatist of the late fourth century BC was the Athenian playwright Menander. During the course of his writing career, this prolific author — he wrote more than 100 plays — almost single-handedly redefined the very nature of Greek comedic theater with an innovative kind of work that eventually would come to be known as New Comedy.

In Menander's plays, traditional Greek theater took on a character that was more complex and more subtle. Rather than exploring the epic struggles of armies and heroes or satirizing the contemporary political leaders, his plots revolved around the often humorous domestic drama of everyday life. Although the actors still wore masks *(left)* and many of the characters remained easily recognizable stereotypes, Menander delved deeply into the nature of the individual. "No one is a stranger to me," he once wrote; "character constitutes the kinship." So popular did Menander's work become that scenes from his plays were often reproduced as murals in houses built during the period *(below)*.

complex of palaces, setting them ablaze. Some said Alexander himself, urged on by a Greek courtesan, threw the first firebrand. By next morning, one of the architectural masterpieces of antiquity lay in smoking ruin. What made the incident especially regrettable was that Alexander's attitude toward the Persians had begun to change. Though tolerant of alien laws and customs, Alexander until now had remained purely Macedonian, sharing a camaraderie with his troops. But the sheer immensity of his possessions called for a new approach. He had already had to hire mercenaries from the conquered lands, diluting his army's character. And now, in Persia, he realized that he had to govern not as a king of Macedonia, but as ruler of an empire.

His new role was a source of irritation to his countrymen. He took to wearing Persian clothes — jacket, headband, possibly trousers — garb Greeks regarded as pompous and effete. As he sat on his imperial throne, robes of royal purple flowing from his shoulders, Persian subjects paying obeisance by kissing their own hands before him, perhaps Alexander enjoyed the ceremony too much. Once he suggested that on state occasions his own men offer the same homage. To roughhewn Macedonian troopers, the idea seemed like betrayal. It was quickly dropped.

At the same time that Alexander was adopting Persian ways, he also began trying to Hellenize the Persians. He founded a school where aristocratic Persian youths learned the Greek language and Macedonian military techniques. A Persian nobleman was appointed to the privileged Companion Cavalry. The Macedonian veterans muttered unhappily, but the Persian remained.

By now, Alexander had been four years in Asia; he was twenty-six years old and he had conquered a little over half the Persian empire. It would take him most of the next eight years to subdue the vast eastern expanses that made up the rest. He set out first in pursuit of the elusive Darius and nearly captured him by the Caspian Sea. At this point, Darius was murdered by a rebellious Persian satrap, and Alexander went after the killer. He eventually caught up with the man in the wastes of Turkestan, had him flogged, and turned him over to a Persian court, which sentenced him to death.

Alexander continued eastward into the tortured, stony landscape of Afghanistan. The tribal warlords of Bactria and Sogdiana resisted fiercely. But one by one, Alexander brought them to heel, and in Sogdiana, he married Roxane, the beautiful daughter of a local chieftain and the conqueror's only known female love.

During this campaign, the simmering tensions between Alexander and his Macedonians finally boiled over. At one point, the troops, weary of travel and combat, petitioned to quit and go home; Alexander talked them around. But then a plot on Alexander's life was uncovered. Several officers, including a close childhood friend, were put on trial and executed.

One of the most disturbing incidents occurred in the midst of a drunken Macedonian revel. A supply of fresh fruit had arrived in camp at Samarkand, just in time for the feast of the wine god Dionysus. Among the celebrants in the royal party was Cleitus, an old friend of Alexander's father who once in battle had warded off a blow that would have killed the young king. As the wine flowed, someone sang a ditty that lampooned the older soldiers. Cleitus took offense, leaped to his feet, and poured out his complaints, including his contempt for Alexander's new airs. "Yes, I saved your life," he shouted, "you who call yourself the son of the gods!"

"You scum, do you think you can speak to me like this and not pay for it?" Alexander cried, hurling an apple at Cleitus. Then he rose and reached for his dagger. Officers held Alexander back and pushed Cleitus from the room, but the old man popped back

The snarling leopard ridden by Dionysus in this mosaic from Delos reflects the dual nature of that Greek god, whose popularity rose as Hellenistic culture spread through Alexander's empire. While Dionysus was the god of wine, pleasure, poetry, dance, and the theater, he was also said to be "the eater of raw flesh who delights in the sword and bloodshed."

in by another door, raging "Alas, what evil customs reign in Greece" — a line from Euripides' *Andromache*. The king, now beyond control, seized a spear from one of his guards and ran Cleitus through.

As the old man's life ebbed away, Alexander quickly sobered. In horror and anguish, he pulled the spear from Cleitus's body and tried to turn it on himself. The Companions wrestled him down and carried him to his tent. He remained there for three days, refusing to eat, wracked by tearful remorse. He was finally persuaded to resume his duties by a priest who convinced him that he had slain Cleitus in a fit of madness induced by a god and thus was not responsible.

The next objective was the Indus Valley, and in 327 BC Alexander and his forces traversed the snowy passes of the Hindu Kush and dropped down into it. By now the army that he was leading was huge: perhaps as many as 120,000 infantry, 15,000 cavalry, and untold provisioners, armorers, administrators, civil servants, and other camp followers.

His desire for conquest was reinforced by his scientific curiosity. Ahead of him lay India, with its monkeys and elephants, its rubies and gold, its steaming jungles and dusty plains, the farthest known reaches of mankind. Beyond the distant Ganges River, at the land's end — or so everyone believed — was the encircling World Ocean. Alexander was determined that he would wet his feet in it.

It was one ambition he was never to realize. The Indian campaign proved unexpectedly demanding, with monsoon weather, increasingly restive troops, and some of the heaviest fighting yet. At the Hydaspes River, Alexander confronted a huge force led by the king of Lahore, whose units included an intimidating squadron of 200 war elephants. The invaders forded the river at night in a thunderstorm and attacked at dawn. The battle raged throughout the day, with awful slaughter on both sides, until a cavalry charge from an unexpected quarter drove the Indians back into their own stampeding elephants. Alexander held the field, but it was an expensive victory.

By the time the army had marched another 200 miles, morale was low and energies exhausted. The troops refused to go on. Alexander took to his tent. When, three days later, he emerged and agreed to turn for home, jubilant shouts rang through the camp.

"Alexander," the soldiers cried, "has allowed us, but no other, to defeat him."

The trek back was arduous. The army traveled in three contingents: one north through the mountains, another by ship across the Indian Ocean and into the Persian Gulf, and the third through the sun-bleached southern deserts. Alexander, aching from half a dozen old wounds, sharing dwindling supplies of food and water with his men, led the desert party. The ragged group reached Persia in the autumn of 325 BC and celebrated with seven days of feasting and drinking.

It was now time to consolidate the empire and reconcile the Greek and Persian cultures. At Susa, Alexander took Darius's eldest daughter as his second wife. It was a lavish state wedding designed to confirm his legitimacy in Persian eyes. Eighty of his officers were given noble Persian brides and generous dowries from the state treasury. Another 10,000 Macedonians who had taken Persian concubines were also rewarded, their liaisons made official, their soldierly obligations suspended, and their children accorded special state recognition.

Then Alexander settled down to deal with the tasks of governing. He issued coins, attended to the army's needs, built a merchant marine, revamped taxes, opened roads, dug irrigation canals, and planned a maritime expedition to explore the Arabian coast. But one June day in 323 BC, while inspecting a drainage project in the Euphrates swamps, he was bitten by an infected mosquito and contracted a fever.

Over the next few days the fever mounted until he was forced to his couch, barely able to speak. One by one his captains filed past, offering last farewells. Alexander acknowledged each sorrowing face. Someone bent down to ask when commemorative rites should be held. "When you are happy," Alexander whispered. Then he closed his eyes and was gone.

Few men changed the world so profoundly. In his brief reign — scarcely thirteen years — Alexander conquered more territory than any other warrior before or since. In his epic march across Asia, he pulled a vast tide of humanity in his wake, not only soldiers but a massive influx of traders, administrators, and ordinary settlers. He vastly broadened the ancient world's horizons, mixing races and cultures, carrying civilization into a new, more cosmopolitan age.

Much of this new outlook came about through the cities Alexander founded. Each was a bit of Greece transplanted to foreign soil. Streets followed a typical grid pattern, as logical and balanced as the Greek mind. There were theaters for dramatic festivals, gymnasia and stadiums for competitive sports, temples to Zeus and Athena, colonnaded markets, and assembly halls where citizens elected local leaders and debated civic affairs. Visitors from Greece felt thoroughly at home.

New prosperity spread across the map. Alexander put much of the captured Persian gold and silver into circulation. The immediate result of this sudden flood of new money was widespread inflation. But more money meant more trade, and eventually it brought a once-stagnant economy to life. A steady program of public works — new roads, canals, and irrigation systems — added to the general industriousness.

Alexander's body was scarcely cold before his officers began quarreling over control of the empire. When asked on his deathbed to name a successor, Alexander is said to have mumbled "the strongest." The struggle to claim that distinction lasted two generations, and during its course the empire broke apart. The eastern possessions in India and Afghanistan were among the first to go, reverting fully to their local rulers. The Greek city-states soon were engaged in their old disputes. Eventually most of them

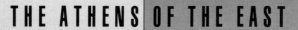

THE ATHENS OF THE EAST

Although Alexander's empire fragmented following his death, his legacy survived in the flourishing Hellenistic kingdoms of Asia Minor. The most impressive of these was Pergamum, whose acropolis of the same name is seen in this artist's reconstruction. The storied city stood on a mountaintop twenty miles from the Aegean.

King Attalos I, who ruled from 241 to 197 BC, determined to make his capital city "the Athens of Asia Minor" with a massive rebuilding project. A prosperous economy made it possible for Attalos and his successors to employ some of the finest architects in the Hellenistic world. The monumental structures that rose on the Acropolis of Pergamum were believed by many to be superior to those of Athens itself.

In addition to the massive royal palace, the buildings included the Temple to Athena, which housed an impressive art collection, and a library that was second in size only to that of Alexandria in Egypt. A theater seating 10,000 people sloped down to the stoa, a column-lined promenade that looked out over the plain below.

sorted themselves into two new groupings, the Aetolian and Achaean leagues, but their former brilliance and strength had faded.

The remainder of the empire was portioned out among Alexander's top generals. Initially, the plan was to hold the lands in trust for his two legitimate heirs: an epileptic half brother in Macedonia and an infant son named Alexander, born to Roxane. But the arrangement was doomed from the start. The generals proceeded to go at each other tooth and nail, grabbing land, trading territories, shifting sides, plotting assassinations, and betraying friends. Roxane and the young Alexander were murdered; so were most of the dead king's other close relatives. When the first line of generals died out, their sons continued the fight. But eventually new boundaries were drawn.

By the early decades of the third century, the empire had split into Greek fragments — consisting of leagues, petty kingdoms, and city-states — and three large hereditary kingdoms: Egypt, ruled by the heirs of Ptolemy I; Macedonia, under the descendants of the general Antigonus; and the vast, sprawling, heterogeneous domains of the Seleucids, stretching from Asia Minor in the west through Syria and Mesopotamia to the deserts of Persia and beyond. Each kingdom developed its own special character. But the crosscurrents stirred by Alexander swept through all three, uniting them in a Greco-Asiatic cultural mix known as Hellenism.

The Ptolemies of Egypt had the easiest time. Ptolemy I, childhood friend of Alexander — and also his first biographer — seized the Nile kingdom at the conqueror's demise. He was blessed by a relatively unified realm with clearly defined borders and an ingrained local tradition of respect for high authority. The Ptolemies filled the ancestral seat of the pharaohs, held absolute power, and were worshiped as gods. In time the Ptolemaic rulers would marry their own sisters, repeating an old pharaonic pattern that enhanced the myth of family divinity. The Ptolemies nonetheless remained powerfully Greek. Thousands of Greeks flooded into Egypt to build cities, man armies and navies, conduct trade, and fill posts in the national bureaucracy. A two-tiered society developed, with an aristocracy and professional class composed mostly of Greeks or Macedonians and a huge Egyptian peasantry.

The crowning distinction of Hellenistic Egypt was Alexandria, which grew into the greatest Western metropolis of the age. Government palaces and administration halls were located there, along with splendidly appointed theaters, stadiums, and other public structures. Cargo from all over the Hellenistic world poured in through Alexandria's seaport: timber from Macedonia and Lebanon, copper from Cyprus, wine from Syria, olive oil from Athens, purple dye from Lebanon. The cargo ships left bearing Egypt's own exports — linen, glass, and papyrus — along with luxury items brought across the desert by caravan. The rest of Africa and Ethiopia provided gold, ivory, and emeralds; pearls came from the Red Sea, myrrh and frankincense from Arabia.

The Ptolemies were ardent patrons of art and learning, and scholars from the Greek world were invited to Alexandria at state expense. The city's library, with its estimated 700,000 manuscripts on papyrus and parchment, was a repository of all Greek knowledge and literature. Science and mathematics flourished. The geometer Euclid lived there. So did Eratosthenes, who calculated the circumference of the earth by the shadows of sticks (he came within 15 percent of the actual distance). And there was Archimedes, perhaps the most inventive of all, who devised a water screw that would still be used two millennia later by Egyptian farmers to irrigate their fields, who emerged from his bath one day with a foolproof method of assaying gold, who invented the pulley and explained the lever.

Having killed his wife, a Gallic chieftain turns his sword on himself rather than surrender to the victorious forces of Attalos, King of Pergamum. The Pergamese triumph over the Gauls in 230 BC was hailed throughout the Hellenistic world, and it confirmed Attalos as the most influential ruler in Asia Minor.

The kingdom of Macedonia was the smallest of the three Hellenistic realms, and it soon ceased to be the prize that it had once seemed. Stripped of its possessions, poor in resources, it reverted to the archaic patterns and parochial concerns of a previous era.

The founder of the third Hellenistic dynasty, Seleucus I Nicator, acquired the bulk of Alexander's empire, and with it the problems of ethnic diversity. Governor in Babylon when the empire was split, Seleucus enlarged his holdings by capturing the Iranian plateau and the eastern provinces, then Asia Minor. He and his successors allowed a certain amount of local expression. The Semitic areas of Mesopotamia enjoyed a cultural renaissance, with a revival of cuneiform writing and the religions of Baal, Marduk, and Jehovah. At the same time the Seleucids continued founding Greek cities, such as Antioch.

But the sprawling agglomeration of principalities and ethnic groups that made up the Seleucid kingdom proved to be ungovernable. A new warrior tribe rose from obscurity on the Iranian plateau, the Parthians, who began carving out their own imperial sphere. Large chunks of Anatolia broke off as local satraps declared independence: Armenia, the Black Sea nations of Bithynia and Pontus, and the cities of Ionia, including Pergamum, which became one of the great cultural centers of its day.

Even the Seleucids' occasional successes often turned sour, as when Antiochus III snatched Palestine from the boy king Ptolemy V in 199 BC. The region remained quiet enough for thirty years, until Antiochus IV decided to brighten the city of Jerusalem with a gloss of Hellenistic culture. His reforms so scandalized the Jews that the tiny nation rebelled, igniting a spark that would burn in Jewish memory for two millennia.

Most cities welcomed Hellenism, however. Because of it, educated men throughout the ancient world spoke one language — a common Greek known as Koine. Business was conducted in Koine, laws were passed in it, and books written in it, including all the New Testament and much of the Old Testament. Greek architects, sculptors, artisans, and goldsmiths left their imprint from the Apennines to the Himalayas. Greek-style jewelry was worn in Siberia, and on the Indian subcontinent some statues of the Buddha wore Greek clothing and posed with an elegant Aegean grace.

The Asian currents that flowed west were also significant, including strains of deep and often fervid mysticism. The mystery religions of Thrace and Asia Minor had long been popular among Greeks. Now the Persian god Mithra, with his firm insistence on unswerving duty, gained favor among army officers. His cult, which employed secret rites of baptism and rebirth long before Christianity began, would eventually be carried through the Roman Empire by soldiers. Another pervasive faith was the Egyptian belief in Isis and Horus, holy mother and tender babe, and in the father Osiris, resurrected from the dead. It, too, was to spread throughout the Mediterranean world.

The Hellenistic kingdoms survived for well over a century, tied together by common bonds of language, culture, and trade. But gradually they grew weaker. The centralized bureaucracy of Egypt became ever more rigid and cumbersome. In Asia, the Seleucid holdings continued to drop away; dynastic struggles exhausted the royal house, and the kingdom was reduced to a minor power centered on Antioch, in Syria. Deep economic divisions cut across society, splitting the world horizontally: An educated, Hellenized upper class presided uneasily over a restive and impoverished mass of native peasants, laborers, and slaves. By about 200 BC, there was little left of Alexander's once great empire. But aggressive newcomers from the west were reaching out to construct an empire of their own. Rome, fast rising to power, was ready to start collecting the pieces of Alexander's Hellenistic world.

EMBLEMS OF MAJESTY

Four years after the death of Alexander the Great, a group of his former officers set aside their feuding long enough to honor the spirit of the conqueror. They assembled before a golden throne that held Alexander's crown, scepter, and diadem. Offering sacrifices in the presence of these symbols of his might, the rivals appealed to Alexander for guidance "as if he were alive," one chronicler wrote. "It was as if a god were leading them on."

Whatever wisdom the officers gleaned from this remarkable ritual, it was not enough to forestall their bloody contest for personal control of Alexander's empire. Still, the incident was a striking demonstration of the enduring mystique of the conqueror's regalia — an aura that would also surround the emblems of other empire builders in the centuries to come. Such emblems, made of gold, marble, jade, and other precious and enduring materials, were seen as extensions of a great man's being, distillates of power that outlasted his earthly term.

In designing such symbols, imperial artists of the era sometimes harked back to the divine attributes of ancient kings. The emperors of China's Han dynasty, for instance, saw themselves as the rightful heirs of the "Sons of Heaven," who had ruled the land in an earlier millennium. Artisans at the Han court obliged their masters by carving jade rings *(page 41)* — traditional symbols of the king's heavenly nature — to be deposited in the royal tombs. In the Near East, the Parthian rulers and their succes-

sors, the Sassanians, appropriated the tokens of the great Persian kings of old and laid claim to the personal support of the chief Persian deity, Ahuramazda. And Caesar Augustus, Rome's first emperor, was fascinated by the legends of Egypt's pharaohs: He took the sphinx, sacred guardian of the pyramids, as one of his personal emblems.

Along with references to the mystical powers of bygone rulers, the empire builders had recourse to an even older set of symbols — the fierce images of fabled predators. Roman legions raised high the eagle, while Indian emperors took the lion as a totem *(above),* and Chinese kings flaunted the serpent or dragon.

Ironically, this resort to archaic symbols of might came at a time when philosophers everywhere were questioning the pretenses of the powerful. Some rulers themselves had reservations about the homage paid them. Alexander, schooled by the skeptical Aristotle, remarked wryly to his followers after being wounded in battle that they saw on his garments plain blood, not the mythical "ichor which flows in the veins of the blessed immortals." And the Indian emperor Asoka, for all his worldly accomplishments, was mindful of the Buddhist masters, who saw earthly ambition as a wellspring of sorrow. Yet the demands of holding together a vast realm left most rulers little time for modesty or misgivings. Empires demanded majesty, and majesty required awesome symbols — regalia to dazzle the eye and mute the questioning voice.

SYMBOLS OF THE GREEK KINGS

Alexander, astride Bucephalus *(left)*, overwhelms hooded Persian troops in a relief from the sarcophagus of the king of Sidon, a vassal of the conqueror.

Alexander inherited a taste for the trappings of power from his father, Philip II, portrayed at far lower right on a gold medallion. Philip cultivated a grand image, and his minions stocked the royal tombs in Macedonia with gleaming treasures that recalled the lavish grave goods of the ancient Mycenaeans. The richest of the royal crypts, believed to be the resting place of Philip himself, contained a gilded silver diadem *(near right)* with an adjustable clasp. (Alexander would wear a similar headband to proclaim his kingship.) After Philip was cremated, his bones were placed in a golden chest *(upper right)*, its lid embossed with a dazzling sunburst. Purple cloth was used to shroud the royal remains, fulfilling to the letter a ritual described in the *Iliad* by Homer, who told how the comrades of the slain Trojan prince Hector gathered up his "white bones and placed them in a golden urn, covering them over with soft purple robes."

TOKENS OF ASIAN ROYALTY

Sassanian victor Ardashir I gets a ring of command from the god Ahuramazda (right), in a scene carved around AD 230 near the tomb of Persia's King Darius I.

The rulers of Asia employed religious emblems along with earthly symbols of power to bolster their authority. The Indian emperor Asoka, who reigned in the third century BC, erected polished sandstone columns throughout his realm; regal lions atop the monuments (center) looked toward the four corners of Asoka's empire, while a wheel below each animal symbolized the doctrine of the Buddha — the vehicle to salvation. In China, late in the second century BC, the Han prince Liu Sheng went to his grave with a jade charm (far right) featuring two rampant dragons standing tail to tail atop a sacred bi, or ring of heaven — a token of the bond between the celestial spirits and their rightful representatives on earth. The lesser lords of China too had emblems of command. The Han emperor allowed the king of Dian to have a golden seal with a snake for a handle (near right). Its stamp lent force to the king's messages.

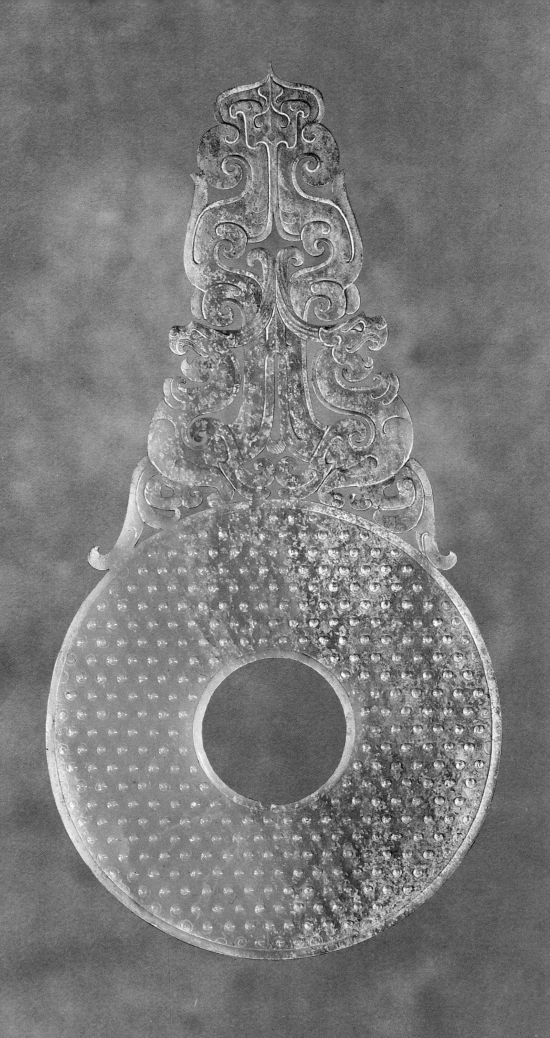

IMAGES OF ROMAN MIGHT

An onyx cameo made about AD 10 shows Augustus being crowned with a wreath near a helmeted goddess embodying Rome.

To convey their leaders' newfound majesty, the artists of imperial Rome looked to the example of the Greeks and adopted a number of their symbols. For centuries, winners at Greek festivals had been crowned with wreaths of olive or laurel — plants sacred to the gods. The Romans accorded the same tribute to their triumphant emperors; wreaths can be seen in the cameo above, around Augustus's brow in the gold coin at near right, and in the claws of the onyx eagle at far right. Similarly, the Romans took the Greek goddess Nike as the model for their winged Victory *(center);* reliefs celebrating imperial campaigns sometimes placed Victory by the emperor in his chariot. The eagle itself — shown at Augustus's feet above — was a lofty symbol, linked with the Greek god Zeus and his Roman counterpart, Jupiter. Just as important to Roman troops, who followed eagle standards, was the bird's gift for swooping down on its prey.

THE GRANDEUR OF IMPERIAL ROME

In its golden age, imperial Rome was a study in sharp contrasts. It was a city of grandeur and squalor, of refined luxury and barbaric savagery, of lofty ideals and low intrigue. The center of the greatest empire in the world, Rome harbored in its heart the ills that would bring about its own decline and fall.

But the magnificence of the city in the first and second centuries AD effectively concealed the signs of weakness. Sprawling across its seven hills east of the yellow Tiber, Rome was a wonder, built on a scale that must have awed anyone who saw it for the first time. At the center was the forum, a complex of great squares bounded by colossal temples and miles of colonnaded markets and overshadowed by the palaces of the emperors on the Palatine Hill. In the forum was the tomb of Romulus, the legendary founder of the city. And there, too, stood the golden milestone that marked the very center of the empire. The distances on every road that led to Rome were measured from it.

All around the forum stood the public buildings of the city, built of travertine (limestone from nearby quarries), of marble, and of brick, their very size a proclamation of wealth and power. To the south of the forum lay the Circus Maximus, one of at least five in Rome where chariot races were held. It could seat 250,000 spectators. To the east the colosseum loomed, offering space for 50,000 people to watch the bloody spectacles provided for their amusement, spectacles whose statistics speak of ferocious extravagance: In one day, 5,000 exotic animals — tigers, bears, elephants, buffalo, rhinoceros — were slaughtered there; in the course of one contest, 350 pairs of gladiators fought to the death in the arena (a word that comes from the Latin *harena,* the sand that was spread after each event to soak up the blood). And farther out stood the public baths — about 170 of them, the finest built by emperors such as Nero, Trajan, and later, in the early third century AD, Caracalla. The baths, too, astonished by their size and splendor. The largest had room for 3,000 people, who for a tiny fee were offered marble gymnasiums for ball playing and wrestling, gardens for walking, libraries and reading rooms, and the baths themselves — steam rooms, dry heat rooms, hot pools, and cold pools.

Such public pleasures provided necessary relief for Romans. A million people resided in the city. Not even a twentieth of them — the very richest — lived in private houses. These turned windowless walls to the dusty streets; within the walls the rooms were grouped around sunny atriums and cool gardens. The houses had their own water supply, their own baths and toilets. Everyone else lived in brick or frame tenements up to four or five stories high, called insulae — "islands" bounded on each side by streets. The insulae were warrens where people slept four or five or more to a small room. The buildings were noisy. Their first floors were lined with shops, and during the day the shopkeepers spread out their wares there — making the narrow streets almost

Beginning as a small city-state on the Tiber, Rome expanded relentlessly after 400 BC. By 250 BC, the Romans controlled most of Italy and were locked in a struggle with Carthage for mastery of the western Mediterranean. A century later, Carthage lay in ruins, and Roman forces had pushed through Greece into Asia Minor. Military success heightened political tensions in Rome; in 45 BC, Julius Caesar capitalized on his triumphant northern campaigns by seizing absolute power. Caesar's successors extended the empire until it reached its zenith *(medium brown)* early in the second century. Lower Mesopotamia remained a contested area between the Romans and the Parthians.

impassable — and loudly conducted business. Because of the congestion, wheeled traffic was forbidden in the city during the day. So the night air echoed with the clattering of supply carts on the paving stones and the shouts of the drivers jockeying for road room. The insulae were also frequently filthy. Water was piped into the first floor in some; people who lived in the rickety upper stories had to lug water up the stairs or pay water carriers to do it. And there was no plumbing for wastes. People used public toilets, some with seats arranged in semicircles to facilitate conversation. Or they used jars set on the street outside the many fullers' shops: Urine was used in the treatment of wool. Or they simply dumped pots of excrement out the windows. The situation was bad enough that damages were assessed against offenders to reimburse passersby injured by such missiles.

Still, Rome was also a city of flowers and gardens. Even the apartment dwellers brightened their windowsills with flowerpots. Festivals were gay with flowers, and there were parks and shady gardens to provide ease from the hot Italian sun.

And the city was rich, in necessities and luxuries. Its water came from the regions around it, piped in through eight great aqueducts. Much of its food and other supplies came from farther away, pouring in primarily to the port of Ostia, twelve miles downriver at the mouth of the Tiber, and brought to the city by barge. Some were essentials: From Italy came wine, fruit, tiles, and bricks; from Sicily, Africa, and Egypt, grain; from Spain, oil and lead; from Gaul, timber, wool, and venison; from Egypt, papyrus; from Greece and Numidia, marble. Some were treasures: Spain sent silver and copper; Africa, ivory; Dalmatia and Dacia, gold; the British Isles, tin; the Baltic, amber; Phoenicia and Syria, glass; India, spices, coral, and jewels; China, silk.

And from every region of the known world came slaves, the chief booty of war. Stripped naked, chained, and marked on the feet with white chalk, with placards around their necks to identify their countries of origin, they were sold at public auction in Rome. It is estimated that at the height of the empire, slaves made up 400,000 of the million inhabitants of the city.

No other society depended so much on slave labor as did Rome in this era. Slaves built the mighty temples and served as attendants in them; they constructed the palaces of the rulers. They farmed the rich people's enormous country estates, served in their great houses, and tutored their children. Slaves were the potters, the jewelers, the garment makers, the shoemakers. Slaves formed the bureaucracy that administered the government of the Roman Empire.

This left the Roman masses with little opportunity for work and chronically poor. To keep them quiet, the emperors provided bread and circuses. Free grain was distributed to as many as 320,000 citizens. And on more than ninety holidays a year, the state or wealthy individuals provided extravagant entertainments — races, animal slaughters, and gladiatorial contests.

As for the rich, they kept apart in their handsome houses and — when they wished to escape the heat and dust of Rome — in villas at such pleasant retreats as Herculaneum and Pompeii. These villas were estates of superb style and comfort, as can be seen in a letter from the orator Marcus Tullius Cicero to his brother, who was traveling in Gaul. "All's right on your estate," Cicero wrote. "Nothing left to do but the baths and a promenade and the aviary. The paved colonnade gives dignity. The columns have been polished and the handsome curve of the ceiling will make it an excellent summer room. . . . Your landscape gardener has won my praise; he has enveloped everything in ivy — even the Greek statues seem advertising it. It's the coolest, greenest retreat.

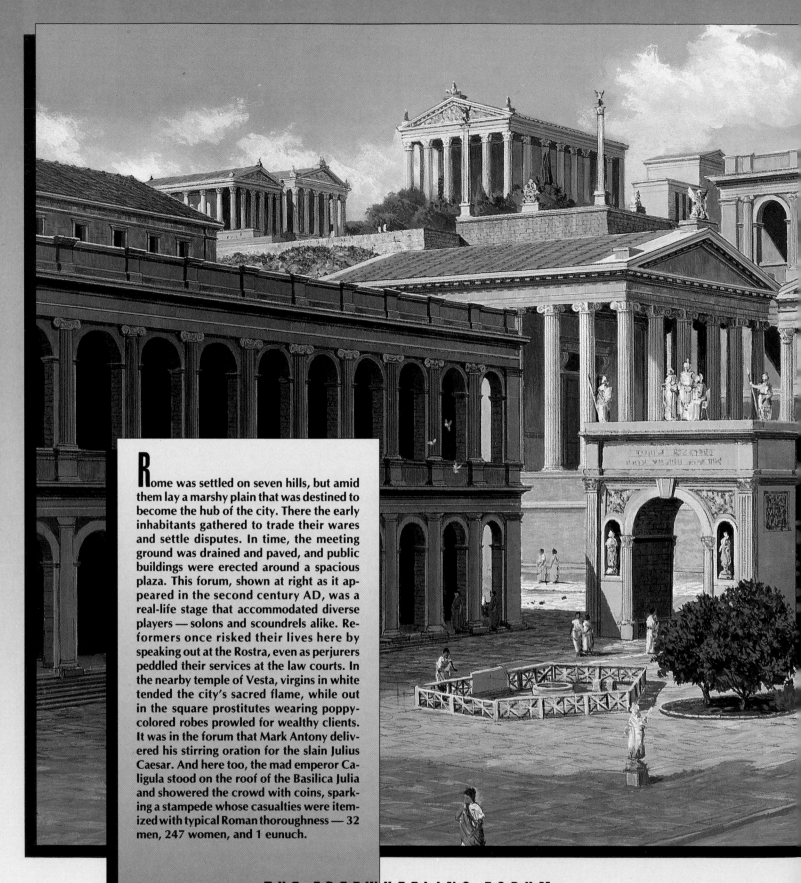

Rome was settled on seven hills, but amid them lay a marshy plain that was destined to become the hub of the city. There the early inhabitants gathered to trade their wares and settle disputes. In time, the meeting ground was drained and paved, and public buildings were erected around a spacious plaza. This forum, shown at right as it appeared in the second century AD, was a real-life stage that accommodated diverse players — solons and scoundrels alike. Reformers once risked their lives here by speaking out at the Rostra, even as perjurers peddled their services at the law courts. In the nearby temple of Vesta, virgins in white tended the city's sacred flame, while out in the square prostitutes wearing poppy-colored robes prowled for wealthy clients. It was in the forum that Mark Antony delivered his stirring oration for the slain Julius Caesar. And here too, the mad emperor Caligula stood on the roof of the Basilica Julia and showered the crowd with coins, sparking a stampede whose casualties were itemized with typical Roman thoroughness — 32 men, 247 women, and 1 eunuch.

THE FREEWHEELING FORUM

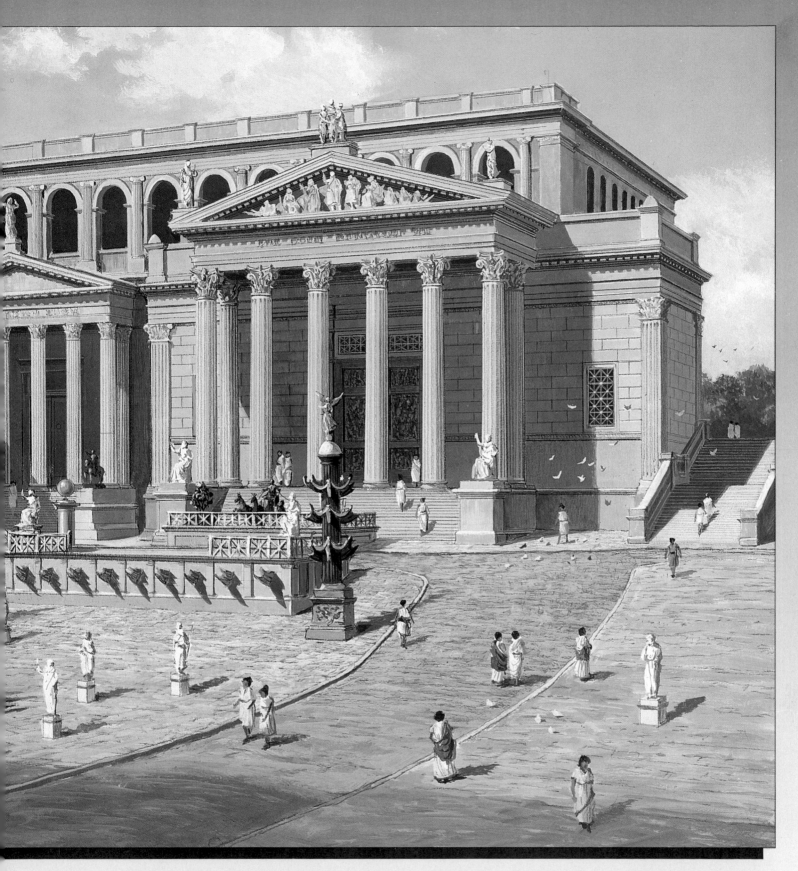

The Rostra stands at the Forum's center, flanked by the Arch of Tiberius; from left to right are the Basilica Julia and temples to Saturn, to the deified Vespasian, and to Concord.

Statues, wrestling ground, fish pond, water system — all are fine.'' The people who lived in houses like this ate from silver dishes and drank from goblets of gold. They dined on boar, venison, and suckling pig — in addition to such exotica as dormice, ostriches, and peacocks — and they drank wine chilled by snow and ice that had been brought from distant mountains and preserved in cool cellars.

Yet the ruling class of imperial Rome existed at the brink of disaster. Rome had begun, Romans liked to think, as a republic guided by a Senate, but at the height of its power, the senators and their colleagues answered not to elected leaders but to emperors — some capable, some incapable, some clearly mad — who ruled with absolute authority for life. As a class these people lived in fear of the emperors above them, of the masses of slaves and mobs of poor below — and of the Roman army, which had become a powerful and dangerous body in its own right.

The threads of military crisis, political strife, and social stress that formed this tapestry of glory and grime stretched back to the earliest years of Rome itself. By 400 BC, the Latin city had been a republic free of its ancient Etruscan kings for almost a century. Loosely allied with other small, nearby states, it was growing in strength, but it was still vulnerable to its neighbors and to adversaries farther away: In 390 BC the city had been invaded and sacked by Celtic tribesmen from Gaul.

Yet in little more than a hundred years after that, the Roman Republic would bring under its control nearly all of the Italian peninsula. Then, as much by reason of their perseverance as because of their prowess at arms, the Romans would endure and eventually emerge victorious from a long and grueling series of wars that left them masters of the Mediterranean world.

These were the Punic wars, named after *Punica*, the Latin word for Phoenician, against the Phoenician empire of Carthage. They were a triumph for the young republic. The irony was that victory and the conquest of the Mediterranean unleashed the insidious forces that would cause the republic's collapse, giving rise to the astonishing synthesis of wealth and poverty, genius and madness, rhetoric and riot, law and disorder that was imperial Rome.

Between them, the republic and its imperial successor would create an empire that reached from Egypt in the south to Britain in the north, from the Atlantic shores of Spain in the west to the Caspian beaches in the east, embracing forty-three provinces and blanketing some two million square miles on three continents. Together, and each in its own way, the Rome of the republic and the Rome of the emperors represent an enduring legacy to the world.

The early Roman republic was aristocratic, not democratic. That is to say, society was divided — as Latin society had been from time immemorial — into two classes: patricians, who were members of perhaps fifty clans, and plebeians, or commoners, whose ancestry lay outside the charmed circle. At first the patricians had held all government power in Rome: They formed the Senate, which varied in size from some 300 to about 1,000. (The Senate was originally a gathering of heads of families, or *patres familiarum*, from which the word patrician derives.) Executive authority was vested in two consuls who were elected for one-year terms. During times of crisis a temporary dictator could be appointed to serve for as long as six months.

The patricians exerted control over society in other, subtler ways, through the paternalistic, hereditary system of *clientela*, in which plebeians pledged to support particular patrician patrons in return for protection and advancement: The patrician's role was such that he was pledged to consider the needs of his plebeian clients before those of his relations by marriage.

But the plebeians, powerless and frequently victimized by their patrician masters, had seethed with discontent. The result had been a continuing political conflict, known as the Struggle of the Orders, in which the plebeians fought to limit the power of the patricians and expand their own. Rich plebeians — and it was possible for a commoner to get rich through trade — tended to lead the movements. They wanted a share of the status and power of the patrician leaders. Poor plebeians, often left landless by almost constant warfare, wanted laws that would protect them against exploitation and abuse. Both of these groups grew desperate during recurring crop failures and famines.

Eventually the plebeians had formed their own assemblies and elected tribunes who could defend the rights they had as Roman citizens against infringement by patricians. Rioting and striking, they had forced the adoption of a written law code, another form of protection. And by 367 BC, they forced the acceptance of a sweeping set of reforms. The measures somewhat softened the pitiless old laws that had allowed debtors and their inheritors to be placed in what was virtually slavery. They also stipulated that at least one of the two men elected annually to Rome's highest magistracy, the consul-ship, must be plebeian.

In the years that followed, the practice of sharing power with the plebeians was gradually extended to other political offices and even to priestly orders. Not only the top office holders but also their direct descendants automatically became eligible for membership in the Senate, where Rome's real power still resided. For that reason, the patrician monopoly in that august body was diluted by a steady infiltration of leading plebeian families. The result was an elite of *nobiles* with mixed patrician and plebeian antecedents. Yet once a plebeian family was admitted to the circle of the new nobility, it naturally tended to take on attitudes as conservative as the bluest-blooded of the old patriciate. In short, far from giving in to the demands of the plebeian movement, the patricians simply absorbed the richest and most ambitious of the plebeians. This gradual resolution of the struggle between the orders meant Rome could unite against her external enemies.

There was no lack of enemies — and Rome was geared to find and meet them. By long tradition, the society was militaristic. Every property-owning Roman citizen (only men were citizens) between the ages of seventeen and forty-six was expected to serve in the army, and this was both an obligation and a privilege. For young aristocrats, the army was preparation for high position: The governmental offices were also military ones; the armies were led by the elected consuls. For aristocrats, military victories meant triumphal processions and increasing wealth from the spoils of war. For the poorer Romans, military service could be ruinous. All soldiers had to pay for their own armor; their wages were barely enough to support a man on a campaign. In addition, small farmers had to neglect their lands while they were at war. Crops failed. The men borrowed to keep their families and their farms going, but then often had to sell their land to pay their debts.

Yet the Roman soldiers' skill and discipline were legendary. So ferocious were they, it was said, that when they sacked a city, they killed even the animals.

Formidable though it was, the army was by no means invincible — and its troubles often began at the top. Even when the consuls' military skills matched their political talent, their one-year term of office could be ruinous to any sort of strategic continuity.

In the course of their constant campaigning, the Romans suffered many major reverses. Yet they were extraordinary in their resiliency, and although they frequently lost their battles, they invariably won their wars.

The earliest victories were close to home. Since 496 BC, Rome had been the leading partner in the military confederation of Latin towns known as the Latin League after Latium, the volcanic plain on the western coast of central Italy. By 340 BC, most of the members of the league, fearing that Rome meant to dominate them completely (as she had centuries before, under the Etruscan kings) joined with several non-Latin tribes to wage war on Rome.

Within three years, Rome had conquered the upstarts, gaining control of western Italy from the Tiber south to Campania. Although the Romans had not the slightest semblance of a master plan for conquest, they were endlessly suspicious of the states that surrounded their growing Italian domain. Rather than waiting to be attacked, they

A provincial farmer bearing a basket of grapes and a rabbit on a pole follows his cow to market past rural shrines — including an enclosure for a sacred tree *(right)* and a small sanctuary for a nature goddess *(center)*, its high offering table laden with fruit. Traditionally, the Romans regarded farming as a noble profession that conferred moral, as well as material, benefits. But by the first century BC, when this relief was carved, there were few self-sufficient farmers left to embody that ideal. Instead, slaves and tenants worked most fields, with absentee landlords reaping the rewards.

reached out and dragged their nearest neighbors into the Roman circle. That, of course, created new next-door neighbors who needed taming. The process of preemptive expansion was thus self-perpetuating. In steady progression, the communities of Italy became members of the Roman household.

Throughout the period of its Italian wars, Rome's treatment of the peoples that it conquered varied considerably. Probably because Rome was entirely lacking in a bureaucracy to administer the affairs of its expanding sphere of control, it struck upon a sort of graded system of governance in which the status of defeated communities was measured by the degree of Roman citizenship that they were granted. So successful was the system that it set the pattern for Rome's treatment of conquered states throughout the succeeding centuries of imperial growth.

The Latin League was dissolved and its former member states were barred from maintaining political relations with one another. Some of the cities near Rome were completely absorbed, and their inhabitants became Roman citizens in the fullest sense, greatly expanding Rome's territory and population — and providing many more soldiers for the army. Others remained nominally independent: They retained the rights of intermarriage (conubium) and of entering into contracts (commercium) with Roman citizens that they had enjoyed under the old Latin League. And some states were assigned to a sort of limbo known as civitas sine suffregio — citizenship without suffrage. This less than totally enivable status imposed upon them all the duties of citizenship, including the payment of taxes and military service, but left them deprived of the privilege of voting. Beyond that, a large number of the non-Latins were bound to Rome by treaties of alliance that, although they differed in detail, invariably required that they provide manpower for Rome's armies.

Rome confiscated large amounts of land from nearly all the states it defeated, sometimes as much as one-third of their territory. The seized land either became part of Rome's public acreage, the ager publicus, or was used to found new colonies peopled by transplanted Romans and strategically placed to defend the city. Drawn mostly from the landless poor, the settlers agreed to give up their Roman citizenship in return for the grant of small tracts that each could call his own.

By 290 BC, Rome held a controlling interest in a huge swath of Italy, reaching from southern Etruria to the Bay of Naples and from the Adriatic to the Tyrrhenian Sea. That put the Romans squarely on the threshold of Magna Graecia, the collection of peevish settlements in the foot of Italy's boot that had been colonized by Greeks as early as the eighth century BC.

Like the city-states of the Greek motherland, Magna Graecia was in a weakened condition because of its own internecine quarrels. During the decade following 290 BC, Rome seized the opportunity to intervene in the affairs of several of the cities of Magna Graecia, a move that brought a violent reaction from Tarentum, the strongest of the Greek states in Italy. Tarentum sought help from beyond the Adriatic in the person of King Pyrrhus of Epirus, a powerful state in northwestern Greece.

Pyrrhus wanted an empire in the west. In 280 BC, therefore, he landed in Italy with 25,000 men and twenty elephants. In two great battles, he defeated Roman armies, yet each time he suffered huge casualties of his own. "One more such victory over the Romans," Pyrrhus supposedly said, "and we are utterly undone."

Pyrrhus was prescient: The Romans recovered, the tide of war changed, and in 275 BC the adventuresome Epirote took himself back to the Greek mainland. In 272 BC, Tarentum surrendered to Rome; by 264 BC, the aggressive young republic

A shepherd carries a kid from his flock in a sling — balancing the load with a jug — in this silver statuette of the first century AD. Such engaging portraits, together with the odes of Roman poets, kept alive the notion that rustics led a privileged life. "Let others vainly sail from shore to shore," the poet Claudian wrote. "Their joys are fewer and their labors more."

A ROMAN CHILDHOOD

Unlike the Spartans of old, who instilled a fighting spirit in their offspring from a tender age, the Romans felt that children should be edified and amused before they shouldered serious concerns. Little Romans had toy knights to deploy — like the wheeled horseman below — but they could also feed toy birds or adjust the limbs on terra-cotta dolls. And there was no rigid separation of the sexes. Girls and boys were schooled together, and they played ball games or tossed quoits *(right)* with equal zest.

Childhood ended soon enough, however. Girls as young as thirteen were deemed marriageable — although their prospective husbands might be considerably older. Adolescent boys of high rank were drilled in grammar and rhetoric for a few years to prepare them for public life; others were simply allowed to run free in gangs until their sport grew too rough. Then they might be sent to the army to learn a harder lesson.

had managed to take control of all Italy south of the Po Valley and was well on its way to a major achievement: The creation of a nation from a group of states of different cultures, religions, and languages.

Up until this point, and despite its surge to Italian supremacy, Rome had remained a minor player on the stage of nations. The triumph over Pyrrhus, however, attracted attention in places as far away as Egypt, whose king began an exchange of envoys with the republic.

Of far greater consequence was the fact that from its stronghold in northeast Africa, mighty Carthage frowned upon the rise of a new Mediterranean power.

Carthage, situated on a promontory in the Bay of Tunis only 130 miles from Sicily, had originally been settled by the Phoenicians, and as sailors and maritime merchants the Carthaginians were worthy of their ancestry. By the third century BC their population was triple that of Rome's. Their territory in northern Africa covered 20,000 square miles, where they and their subject peoples cultivated wheat, olives, and fruit, including grapes from which they made wine. The Carthaginians had also won footholds in Spain (which they valued highly for its metals), achieved dominion over Sardinia, and, after centuries of striving, seemed about to achieve hegemony over Sicily, a crucial stepping-stone in their trade routes.

Although an eventual collision between Carthage and Rome was perhaps inevitable, they more or less stumbled into conflict when each was asked to intervene between the Sicilians and mercenaries who controlled the Sicilian city of Messana (later called Messina).

The result, beginning in 264 BC, was the first of the Punic wars — Rome's first step outside Italy. The war was fought mostly at sea, a circumstance that initially put the landlubberly Romans to great disadvantage against the maritime might of the Carthaginians. Although the Romans at the outset possessed no fleet of warships, they built a navy, using as a model a captured Carthaginian quinquereme.

The war was one of attrition that seesawed back and forth for twenty-three years. During that period entire fleets on both sides were destroyed in battle and by storms, rebuilt, destroyed, and built again. In all, the Romans lost an estimated 600 ships and as many as 250,000 men, and the Carthaginians 500 vessels and 210,000 men in naval battles alone. Finally, in a momentous clash of the rival fleets off the western coast of Sicily, the Romans sank fifty enemy ships and captured seventy others. They captured the Carthaginian strongholds in Sicily, and Carthage was forced to sue for peace. Reaping its reward, Rome took over both Sicily, the original cause of contention, and, later, by a piece of trickery, Sardinia and Corsica, thereby making its first overseas acquisitions on the way to empire.

But the Carthaginians rallied with amazing speed. In Africa they had taken control of Algeria and Morocco; using these lands as their base, they invaded Spain, rich in metals and in hardy men of Celtic and Iberian stock to fill the ranks of the depleted army. The leader of the invasion was Hamilcar Barca, a member of one of Carthage's leading families. He entered Spanish waters in 237 BC, bringing with him his nine-year-old son, Hannibal.

In the seventeen years that followed, the Carthaginians conquered most of southern and eastern Spain with its rich mines and rich farmland; they pushed as far north as the River Ebro, near the foothills of the Pyrenees. As their headquarters in Spain, they chose an old Phoenician settlement on the country's east coast; called New

Carthage, this city boasted one of the best harbors in the world. During those years Hamilcar Barca died in battle. His son-in-law succeeded him as leader of the Carthaginian forces in Spain, but not long afterward he was murdered, and command passed to young Hannibal.

Legend had it that the father had sworn the son to vengeance on Rome. Whether that was true or not, Hannibal soon began to move against the Romans. His base at New Carthage was more than 1,000 marching miles from the Italian capital, a distance that even the Romans, sensitive as they always were to their own security, could hardly consider threatening. They did not, however, care to have a former enemy come closer than that, and they therefore concluded a treaty in which Carthage agreed to refrain from crossing the Ebro River.

But Hannibal, vengeful or reckless, did not fear to affront the Romans. He savagely besieged the wealthy city of Saguntum, which, although it was situated some seventy-five miles south of the Ebro and was therefore well within the territory allowed to Carthage, professed to a bond of friendship with Rome. The Romans sent envoys asking Hannibal to cease his attack on Saguntum. He refused. Seriously affronted, Rome then dispatched a delegation to Carthage to demand that the Carthaginians hand Hannibal over to Rome for punishment.

High drama surrounded the delivery of the ultimatum. Facing the Carthaginian senate, an elderly Roman named Fabius Buteo placed his hand on the spot where his toga gathered at his breast; from its folds, he said, he could shake out either peace or war. The Carthaginians left the choice to him. Whereupon Fabius, letting the folds fall, cried: "We give you war!"

So, in March of 218 BC commenced the second and most terrible struggle between Rome and Carthage.

The following month, Hannibal set out on the land route for Rome, leading the finest army Carthage ever had fielded. There were some 46,000 men, including a core of his own light infantry veterans and an exotic array of mercenaries gathered from Iberia and Africa, plus thirty-seven battle elephants (which, in the end, were to play an insignificant role in Hannibal's battles). He meant this war to be fought on Roman soil, thus sparing Spain the devastation of battle; he also expected to find allies among the Gauls and the various Italian tribes conquered by Rome.

Fording the Ebro, trekking over the Pyrenees, floating his elephants by raft across the Rhone, Hannibal reached the grim massif of the Alps, already deep with drifts of snow and lashed by autumnal winds. A cruel fifteen days lay ahead.

Many stories would be told about that journey, about the struggles of the courageous soldiers and bewildered elephants trudging through the snowdrifts along the mountain ledges and narrow defiles. In fact, although the Alpine passes were hard, they provided efficient routes for moving armies from the valley of the Rhone in Transalpine Gaul to the valley of the Po in Cisalpine Gaul, the land at the north end of the Italian peninsula. The Gauls did it regularly. The secret was the support of the inhabitants: Large Gaulish tribes held the Alps, and their guides could take strangers safely through. Hannibal and his men, however, received no aid. The tribesmen constantly attacked with spears and with boulders; the guides who were hired deserted. Blindly, the army struggled on until in September of 218 BC it passed through a 5,400-foot-high gap in the crest of the chain.

By one estimate, Hannibal's army had possessed 38,000 infantry and 8,000 cavalry at the time of the Rhone crossing. Of those, only 20,000 foot soldiers and 6,000 horsemen survived to gaze down upon the Po River valley in Cisalpine Gaul, a region that the Romans, in the aftermath of the First Punic War, had suppressed but by no means subdued. There, a Roman force awaited, keenly aware of the Carthaginian approach — and of their desperate plight. Proclaimed a Roman general: "They are the ghosts and shadows of men already half dead. All their strength has been crushed and beaten out of them by the Alpine crags."

He was badly mistaken. By the end of the following spring, Hannibal's army — greatly reinforced by Cisalpine Gauls who had risen against their Roman oppressor — thrice administered resounding defeats to the Romans in northern Italy. Then, painfully aware that he lacked the heavy equipment necessary for a siege of Rome, Hannibal bypassed the enemy capital and took his army south.

There he hoped to inspire Rome's coerced allies to revolt against their master and join his cause. He said that he had not come to fight against Italians, but on behalf of Italians against Rome. Yet despite his promises of freedom from Rome's rule, Hannibal was low on supplies and had to allow his army to plunder Roman dependencies in southern Italy. The states reacted accordingly; apparently not a single one of them voluntarily joined the Carthaginian cause.

During this period, Rome's temporary military dictator was a crafty old nobleman and former consul named Quintus Fabius Maximus, who soon won the nickname Cunctator — the delayer — for his refusal to meet Hannibal in pitched battle. Instead, Fabius realized that Carthage must eventually lose a long war of attrition fought on Roman soil, and he contented himself by nibbling away at the peripheries of Hannibal's force in countless small actions.

Effective though it was, the Fabian strategy was unpopular among less patient Romans, and in 216 BC they elected a pair of consuls who were both committed to a head-on collision with Hannibal. They got their wish at Cannae, a small fortress and stores depot near the heel of Italy's boot — a position that Hannibal had seized and the Romans needed.

Hannibal's tactics were of classic simplicity. He had studied Roman methods and knew that the enemy would use its 86,000 men — the largest army that Rome had ever put into the field — to lunge at the center of his 50,000 troops. He therefore arranged his front in a long convex arc with a purposely weakened center, and his crack cavalry, backed up by columns of pikemen, on the wings.

Under a blazing August sun, the Romans crashed headlong into Hannibal's center, which predictably gave way, converting the convex crescent into a concave one. As the Romans drove deeper into the pocket, they were surprised to find themselves enveloped by Hannibal's cavalry, who closed in on both flanks and the rear, penning in the Romans so tightly that they did not even have room to swing their swords. Sheer carnage was the result of the double envelopment — a classic tactic that would cause the battle to be studied in military classrooms for millennia thereafter. At least 50,000 Romans were slain and 10,000 more were taken prisoner. It was the greatest military disaster Rome had ever suffered.

In the immediate aftermath of Cannae, as the extent of the Carthaginian victory became clear, the brilliant Numidian cavalry commander, Maharbal, urged that Hannibal march directly against the city of Rome. "Within five days," the Numidian predicted, "you will take your dinner, in triumph, on the Capitol!" When Hannibal refused to make such a move, Maharbal was thoroughly disgusted. "You know, Hannibal, how to win a fight," he announced. "You do not know how to use your victory."

In fact, Hannibal was convinced that Rome's humiliation at Cannae would at last cause its allies to come to his side, and he was right — up to a point. Led by Capua, the most important city of Campania and the second largest in Italy, many of the allies in the South did switch their allegiance. But many others did not, and those of central Italy remained solidly Roman. Thus, with the Romans reverting to the cautious policies of Fabius, the lines were drawn roughly along the Volturno River, 108 miles south of Rome. The Carthaginians remained in southern Italy for thirteen more years, sporadically fighting the Romans, who were rebuilding their strength in the north.

The Romans finally struck back when Publius Cornelius Scipio, whose consul father had been defeated in Hannibal's first Italian skirmish, began aggressive operations in Spain. Scipio succeeded in 209 BC: He captured New Carthage and, over the next four years, conquered all of the Carthaginian territory in Spain. Then, in the spring of 204 BC, he transported his army to North Africa to strike at his enemy's heart. Summoned to defend his homeland, Hannibal at last left Italy, only to suffer a disastrous defeat in the battle of Zama, some seventy-five miles southwest of Carthage, for which the honorific "Africanus" was attached to Scipio's name. The next year, 201 BC, Carthage sued for peace.

As for Hannibal, the brilliant tactician stayed in Carthage for some years as chief magistrate, trying to organize the city to pay the heavy tributes Rome demanded. But the Romans were after him. Denounced for plotting against them, he fled to Syria, then to Bithynia, where he committed suicide by poison in 183 BC just before he was to be turned over to his enemies.

There would be yet another Punic war, but it was of relatively brief duration and ended in 146 BC, when another Scipio, the adopted grandson of Scipio Africanus, burned Carthage, plowed its ashes, and sowed the furrows with salt so that nothing would be able to grow there again. Carthage and the region around it were annexed to Rome as the new province of Africa. As conclusive as that encounter was, it was hardly more than a footnote to the Second Punic War — the conflict that set Rome on the road to world empire.

Not only were the Punic wars responsible for Rome's immediate expansion, as in the conquests of Sicily and Spain, but they also led to later acquisitions needed to protect the new territories. The Cisalpine Gauls to the north, for instance, were a problem during the wars with Carthage, when they enthusiastically sided with Hannibal, and for fifty years afterward; the series of campaigns Rome took to secure its northern borders and protect the routes to newly acquired Spain was long and bitter. The north of Italy was not fully Romanized until 150 BC.

To the west, unruly Spain itself required the continuing presence of the Roman army; in 197 BC the peninsula was formally annexed and divided into the provinces of Nearer and Farther Spain. In the same period, Rome reached out toward the east, going to war against Illyria on the eastern shore of the Adriatic in 230 and 219 BC, using as an excuse piracy and coastal raiding from bases there. Illyria first became a client state, then in 168 BC was broken up into three parts, which were not allowed to cooperate with one another. Macedonia, led by Philip V, a mercurial monarch who dreamed of returning his kingdom to the glory it had known under Alexander the Great, met a similar fate. Philip was bent on expanding his territory in the Balkans and in Greece. Proclaiming that they meant to ensure "freedom for the Greeks," the Romans in 214 BC embarked on a series of Macedonian wars that sputtered on and off for more than

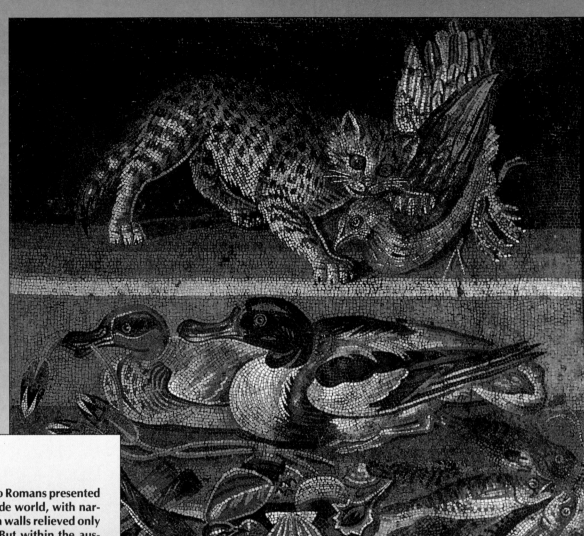

Two panels of a floor mosaic from Pompeii reveal contrasting aspects of nature: a cat pouncing on a partridge and birds perched peacefully on the surface of a marshy inlet rife with fish and flora. The animal figures that graced Roman dwellings were not exclusively decorative: The vestibules of some houses were tiled with portraits of watchdogs *(inset)* as an unmistakable warning to intruders. One such mosaic spelled out the threat in a legend: *Cave Canem* — Beware of the dog.

The houses of well-to-do Romans presented a stark face to the outside world, with narrow entryways and plain walls relieved only sparingly by windows. But within the austere facade lay brighter scenery: wall paintings and mosaics that truly teemed with life. The natural world provided an especially rich subject for the artists who decorated Roman interiors. Animals were rendered with the realistic flair characteristic of Greek art, for freedmen of Greek origin or training dominated the trade; in turn, the artists bequeathed their fine eye for detail to apprentices — slaves who might themselves earn freedom one day and become masters of the craft.

Much of what these artists produced eroded with the Roman Empire. But the creatures portrayed here were preserved by a sudden catastrophe: In AD 79, the eruption of Mount Vesuvius sent a suffocating cloud of ash down on Pompeii, a community of 20,000 people, 120 miles south of Rome. Residents met an agonizing death, but the volcanic debris settled benignly over murals and mosaics — giving a later age an unequaled view of the designs favored in Roman homes.

AT HOME WITH NATURE

The artists who painted on Roman walls portrayed a host of feathered creatures, ranging from poultry *(inset)* to the regal peacock. The peacock was an emblem of the goddess Juno, wife of Jupiter, but that did not prevent the Romans from savoring the bird's flesh. The satirist Juvenal poked fun at the diner who indulged in such a feast before rushing off to the public baths: "You will soon pay for it, my friend, when you take off your clothes and, with distended stomach, carry your peacock into the bath undigested."

Wall paintings sometimes presented domestic vignettes along with glimpses of nature in the wild. At near right, a partridge hangs ready for plucking on a kitchen wall while a live hare — itself destined soon for the pot, perhaps — gnaws avidly on a bunch of grapes. At far right, a cat eyes a trio of birds arrayed around a fountain; such reservoirs stood in the enclosed gardens of many Roman villas.

Painted serpents like the pair here often adorned the Roman lararium, a small indoor shrine where family members made daily offerings to their household gods. The Romans were not alone in associating snakes with the powers responsible for the health and prosperity of the family: On Crete, household snakes were long protected and revered as benevolent visitors from the netherworld.

half a century. They fought first against Philip, then against his son and successor Perseus, and finally against an impostor named Andriscus, who fobbed himself off as a son of Perseus. After its first victories, Rome made Macedonia a client state with a degree of freedom. But continuing resistance in Macedonia led to harsh reprisals. The Romans deliberately destroyed the country's wealth, and divided it into four self-governing republics. Later, Rome reunited Macedonia — as a Roman province, directly ruled by a resident Roman governor.

And in the same period, Asia Minor fell to Rome. It was ruled by Syria's Seleucid king Antiochus III who, like Philip of Macedonia, was heir to a huge kingdom carved out of the old empire of Alexander the Great. And like Philip, Antiochus was restless and expansion minded. In 192 BC he invaded Greece, although Rome, as a warning aimed specifically at him, had declared that country to be free. Rome responded almost immediately. Its legions routed Antiochus at the ancient battle site of Thermopylae, driving him back to Asia Minor. He and his Syrians were pursued by the redoubtable Scipio Africanus, who in this case was under the command of his brother, soon to become Scipio Asiaticus. For the first but by no means the last time, Rome's soldiery set foot on the Asian continent, where it smashed Antiochus at Magnesia and Sipylum near Smyrna. Antiochus III was forced to retire behind the Taurus Mountains and give up all his possessions in Asia Minor. Following their by now familiar practice, the Romans first established client states in Asia Minor and later made most of that region the Roman province of Asia. Eventually, Syria itself was conquered and absorbed by the growing empire as a Roman province.

If the Second Punic War put Rome on the highway to empire, it also set in motion more subtle forces within Italy that would eventually cause the end of the republic.

Hannibal's depredations in southern Italy had laid waste to the farmlands upon which the region's economy depended. Rome, in turn, had confiscated for its public land immense tracts from the Italian communities that had sided with Carthage. Beyond that, the peasant landowners of Rome's Italian allies had provided more than half of the conscripts who fought Hannibal. And during the thirty-three years following his defeat, Rome kept as many as 130,000 soldiers in the field, fighting its foreign wars. More than half of all adult males spent at least seven years in low-paid military service. Their prolonged absences left their little farms neglected, and upon their return they found themselves saddled with debts and entirely unable to maintain their property. The beneficiaries of the peasant plight were, of course, the members of the nobility and wealthy plebeians, who had both the money and the time required to return the ruined lands to productivity.

Ancient custom held that it was beneath the dignity of the Roman elite to earn income through mercantile activities. A direct involvement in commerce was considered sordid to the point that senators were legally prohibited from owning large ships that could be used for trading. At the same time, it was perfectly permissible for an aristocrat to increase his wealth by the acquisition of land. Marcus Porcius Cato, the famous censor — the official who oversaw both the national census and national morals — listed the three best of all possible investments as, first, good pasturelands; second, mediocre pasturelands; and third, poor pasturelands. Through bankruptcies, forced sales, evictions, and sometimes brute force, the magnates took over the peasant farms. More than that, through grants, bribes, and governmental laxness, large-scale landowners usurped immense tracts of the ager publicus.

The result was the growth of super-estates, or latifundia, some of which are known to have bloated to upwards of 400,000 acres. To make matters even worse for Italy's peasants, once they had been dispossessed from their farms they could not even count on finding employment on latifundia, because of the hordes of slaves who by now had become the hallmark of Roman life.

The slaves came by the tens and hundreds of thousands: After the Roman victory over Perseus, for instance, some 150,000 of Macedonia's Epirote allies were taken into slavery in a single day. At the peak of the one-way traffic to Rome, the Greek free port of Delos could handle up to 10,000 slaves daily.

This flood helped shape Rome in the last days of the republic and in the centuries of empire. People comfortably off might own 500 slaves, as the first century AD statesman Pliny the Younger did; the very rich might own 4,000; emperors, 20,000. Many of these slaves, of course, served in the burgeoning Roman bureaucracy or performed the manual labor needed for farming, mining, building, and public works. But this left battalions of household slaves whose jobs, as their funeral inscriptions show, were amazingly specialized: There were slaves to take care of each category of clothing, each kind of eating and drinking vessel, each kind of jewel, not to mention each stage of grooming, each kind of cooking, and every kind of service.

Their treatment varied according to their masters and their jobs, from security and comfort to hideous degradation. The life of an agricultural slave, for instance, was awful, endless drudgery. Legally, a slave's lot was a poor one: The laws showed that Romans feared this captive army. Slaves could be tortured, beaten, and for a variety of crimes, put horribly to death by crucifixion. They could be killed for running away or for trying to pass themselves off as free. If a slave murdered his master, every slave in the household could be executed as an accomplice. How hard their lives could be is shown by laws limiting their maltreatment. It was ruled, for instance, that no slave could be forced to fight as a gladiator and — more pitiably — that it was illegal to kill or abandon slaves who were too old or ill to work. Because of the brutal way slaves were treated, Cato could write, "you have as many enemies as you have slaves." The Romans did not forget it.

Yet in an institutional sense, Roman slavery was extraordinary in at least one respect: Slaves were often emancipated, and upon achieving their freedom, they became Roman citizens, although they were denied certain political offices. Some manumissions doubtless stemmed from the fondness of masters' hearts and were in reward for faithful service. Often, however, slaves were freed as part of the eternal quest for investment possibilities. Freedmen, although citizens, were encumbered by none of the nobility's prohibitions against engaging in commerce. An aristocrat, even while maintaining a polite distance from such tawdry enterprise, might therefore finance a freedman in business in return for a share of the profits. For example, that pillar of Roman rectitude, the censor Cato, used his freedman Quintio as a frontman for a shipping company, from which Cato received a handsome return. Through such practices, former slaves came to occupy an important niche in the Roman economy — generally at the expense of urban citizens who had been born free but poor.

Still, after the slaves themselves it was the rural smallholders

Symbols of mortality abound in a Pompeian mosaic buried along with most of the town's residents in the cataclysmic eruption of Vesuvius. Beneath the skull are a wheel of fortune and a butterfly, emblematic of life's fleeting spirit; the roof above is made up of a carpenter's tools — a square, a level, and a plumb line — to signal that death takes the measure of all things. Such grim reminders encouraged the Romans to make the most of life before it escaped them, an outlook summed up by the proverbial injunction *Carpe diem* — Enjoy today.

The embossed bronze helmet at right was the proud property of a trained Roman gladiator. As illustrated below in a mosaic of the second century AD, such well-armed men might meet each other on an equal footing in the arena, while musicians punctuated the action with fanfare and the strains of a water organ. Feats of deadly skill were only part of the program, though. Unarmed victims were whipped into line (bottom) to face beasts of prey that had been starved for the occasion, and the animals themselves were mercilessly baited.

The blood sports that so enthralled the Romans originated as funeral rites. In the early days of the republic, violent contests between slaves were sometimes staged to mark the death of wealthy nobles. The bouts gave the deceased a blood offering while allowing the potential victims at least a chance for survival. Soon, Roman rulers learned to exploit the allure of such carnage. The aspiring Julius Caesar curried public favor by gathering 640 gladiators in the arena. And the emperor Trajan celebrated his triumph over Dacia in AD 106 by presenting a murderous marathon in Rome's coliseum that lasted for 117 days and involved nearly 10,000 combatants, many captive Dacians. The appeal of such spectacles, which often included animals, was not limited to the rabble. Senators were given prime seats — as were vestal virgins, who watched as the mob clamored for the emperor to spare or condemn a gladiator.

Critics realized that such pastimes — along with their lavish handouts of food — had helped to reduce the average Roman from a good citizen to a jaded spectator. As Juvenal wrote, "The public that once bestowed commands, consulships, legions, and all else, now meddles no more and longs eagerly for just two things — bread and circuses!"

A BRUTAL DIVERSION

who suffered most by the system, and in their despair they flocked to the cities, particularly Rome, in search of work and food for their families. Far from improving their lot, they found themselves packed into the insulae built by noble slumlords along alleys so narrow that an occupant of one flat could reach out the window and shake hands with a neighbor across the passageway. Cheaply constructed, the buildings occasionally collapsed, and a single spark from a charcoal stove could set off a conflagration that consumed acres of similar tinderbox structures.

And so the poor got poorer, the rich got richer, the social chasm deepened, and the potential for violence increased. It came in 133 BC, little more than a decade after the Third Punic War, and the chief victim was a tribune named Tiberius Gracchus, a man of noble lineage. (Among other connections, he was a grandson of the renowned Scipio Africanus.) Gracchus sought to alleviate the misery of the masses, and to create a larger pool of landowners from which to draw men for the army, by means of a land-reform bill aimed at redistributing much of the ager publicus to the poor.

The measure, of course, could hardly have been more obnoxious to the owners of the great latifundia, who dominated the Roman Senate and who suspected that Gracchus was plotting to make himself a popular dictator. It therefore happened that while Gracchus was campaigning for reelection, he and about 300 of his supporters were set upon and clubbed to death by a huge mob led by senators.

Ten years later, his younger brother Gaius Gracchus was elected to the same office and promptly instituted even more sweeping reforms. Reelected once, he was defeated in 121 BC. Later, when Gaius and his supporters demonstrated to protest a Senate action, the Senate instructed Rome's consuls to suppress them by whatever means. As a result, Gracchus and about 3,000 others were seized and put to death.

In the assassination of Tiberius Gracchus, the republic's ruling class for the first time had drawn the blood of a tribune — the plebeians' official representative, whose safety had been guaranteed more than three centuries before. The slaughter of Gaius Gracchus and his followers was yet another stride toward anarchy. "Thereafter," wrote a Roman historian, "civil strife, which in the past had been settled by agreement, was settled by the sword."

The slayings of the Gracchus brothers had revealed a great chasm in Roman society, giving rise to bitterly divided factions even within the nobility itself. On the one hand were the *optimates,* conservatives who yearned for a return to ancient Roman values, who supported traditional property rights and public economy. Ranged against the optimates were the *populares,* political aspirants who, like Tiberius and Gaius Gracchus, appealed to the masses by espousing such causes as land reform and grain distributions. Adding to the political discord was the rising equestrian, or knightly, order, a class composed mainly of men rich enough to be senators but who were not actually members of the Senate.

For the first few years after the death of Gaius Gracchus, the optimates remained in control. After 114 BC, however, a series of military disasters gave the populares their chance. During the Punic wars and the subsequent building of the Roman Empire, the Senate's authority had been hugely enhanced by success. Now, however, consuls sponsored by the Senate botched campaigns in Macedonia, which had been invaded by Thracian tribesmen, and against Germanic barbarians who were threatening Rome's northern territories.

To add to Rome's woes, a North African "client king," a Numidian chieftain named Jugurtha, had taken up arms in an attempt to maintain a degree of independence from his Roman masters. When Rome sent an expedition to tame him, he allegedly bribed a Roman general to make a peace that permitted him to keep his throne. However, word of the deal leaked out, an investigation was begun, and Jugurtha was brought to Rome as a material witness. According to one account, that was a role he did not fancy at all, and he bribed certain senators to excuse him from testifying. Upon departing for home, he supposedly summed up his experience with a scalding comment: "In Rome, all things are for sale."

The episode badly damaged the prestige of the Senate, and in the outraged public clamor that ensued, a most unlikely candidate was elected consul over fierce senatorial objections. He was Gaius Marius, an army veteran of equestrian birth and a champion of the populares, who loathed the optimate nobility. "They despise me for an upstart, I despise their worthlessness," he cried. "They can taunt me with my social position, I them with their infamies."

Between 107 and 100 BC Marius was elected consul for an unprecedented six terms, during which he wrought changes in the basic nature of the Roman army that would, in due course, prove not only fatal to the republic but a plague to the imperial regimes that followed.

Because of the decline in the number of small landowners, who in earlier times had borne the main burden of military service, the army had long been ignoring the ancient property qualification. Marius made the change official and openly recruited his men from the landless and generally jobless Romans who were mobbing the cities. To those who enlisted, Marius held out hopes of sharing in the plunder of war and, after serving for up to twenty years, the possibility of pensions and perhaps even their own patches of land.

Marius thus completed the transformation of the army from a peasant militia, whose members were mostly taking time off from their plows to serve their country, to a professional establishment whose soldiers owed their allegiance less to the Roman state than to the generals upon whose triumphs their fortunes depended. Inevitably, the new army would become a political tool.

But in the hands of Marius, it immediately proved an effective military force. He used it to vanquish Jugurtha and to turn back the Germanic barbarians who had set Rome into such a panic that human sacrifices were made to appease the gods. Yet he was still reviled by Rome's elite, and when the threats to the empire's security ended, so did his usefulness. Without political support, embittered and drinking heavily, Gaius Marius retired to Asia Minor.

But not for long. Rome's Italian allies, who for the most part had remained loyal during the critical days of the war against Hannibal, had long been chafing against their secondary citizenship status. They resented paying for wars that delivered to them no benefits and being affected by political decisions over which they had no control. In 91 BC, after the murder by persons unknown of a tribune who had attempted to give them full Roman citizenship, the allies revolted in what would later become known as the Social War — from the word socii, meaning allies. To meet the emergency, the old warhorse Marius was called back to service, and he was soon in command of the Roman forces in northern Italy; meanwhile, in the south, the army was led by Lucius Cornelius Sulla, who had once been a paymaster under Marius.

Despite Roman military successes, the conflict continued for two years. It ended only when Rome buckled under, granting some of the political demands of the allies. Henceforth, nearly all Italians would be Romans in the fullest sense of the name.

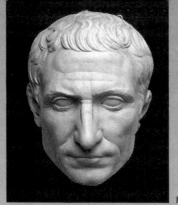

JULIUS CAESAR

THE LEGION

LEGATUS

6 TRIBUNES

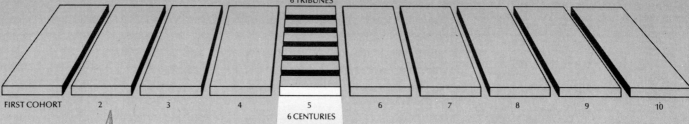

FIRST COHORT   2   3   4   5   6   7   8   9   10

6 CENTURIES

10 CONTUBERNIA (8 MEN EACH)

CENTURION

LEGIONARY

CENTURION

By the time the Social War was over, Sulla was clearly Rome's rising star: In 88 BC he was elected consul and named to command an army being sent against Mithradates VI of the Black Sea kingdom of Pontus. Mithradates and his army had overrun Rome's Asian province and (according to possibly exaggerated reports) slaughtered 80,000 Roman residents in a single day. This time, however, Marius was by no means content to retire, and while Sulla was assembling his army in southern Italy, Marius successfully conspired to have command of the expedition against Mithradates taken away from Sulla and given to himself.

Infuriated, Sulla turned his legions northward — and for the first time a Roman army, its loyalties linked to a general instead of the state, marched upon the city of Rome with violent intent. Marius, who recognized superior power when he saw it, fled to Africa. Sulla entered Rome a winner.

Yet the struggle between Sulla and Marius was far from over. Their personal differences were symbolic of the political forces that were tearing the republic asunder. Marius, still the darling of what one unfriendly Roman called "all the artisans and rustics," was the epitome of the popularis. Sulla, unscrupulous scion of one of Rome's oldest patrician families, was the perfect optimate.

Once Marius had taken to his heels, Sulla set off to squelch Mithradates, a task that took him about four years. During his absence, and with Marius still in exile, Rome's social and political order broke down. Rioters surged through the streets, bloody brawls broke out in the forum, and political assassinations and judicial murders were commonplace. Taking advantage of the chaos, Marius returned to Italy, raised an army of veterans still faithful to him, marched on Rome, and got himself named consul for the seventh time.

Hardly had this term as consul begun, however, than Marius died, leaving the republic to popularis politicians. Their shaky regime came to an end in 83 BC, when Sulla, having at last prevailed over Mithradates, returned to Italy. As he moved on the city of Rome, entire legions of 6,000 men each were enticed by his promise of rewards and went over to his side.

After he had won, Sulla mercilessly eliminated any future threat from the followers of Marius. Once, while Sulla was addressing the Senate, the members were distracted by the rising sound of an uproar in the streets outside. According to Plutarch, Sulla simply "bade the senators to pay attention to his speech and not busy themselves with what was going on outside: some naughty people were being admonished at his orders." In fact, some 6,000 Marians were being put to death.

Now in uncontested power, Sulla arranged for a subservient Senate to declare him Rome's dictator — not for the six-month period that had always been customary in times of deep crisis, but for as long as he cared to hold the office. As it turned out, Sulla tired of the job after only four years. At the end of that time he left for his country estate, where he whiled away the remaining year of his life enjoying the company of his fifth wife and writing poor poetry. He had tried to strengthen the republic by reinforcing the senatorial oligarchy, bringing in several hundred new senators from the equestrian order, but that change did nothing to solve Rome's persistent problems of political preferment and corruption.

By long tradition, noble Romans viewed the holding of public office as less an option than an obligation that went with their patrimony. Moreover, since the republic's earliest days they had adhered to a strict order of promotion by which an aspirant climbed a ladder from the lowliest offices to the judicial position of praetor and finally

The supremacy of Caesar's Rome was maintained by a well-disciplined and highly organized force of professional soldiers known as legionaries. A recruit enlisted for twenty-five years and after a period of arduous training joined one of twenty-eight legions that formed the backbone of the Roman army (chart, opposite). Each legion was commanded by a veteran general, or legatus, with six tribunes — usually young aristocrats — as subordinates. At full strength, a legion consisted of ten cohorts of about 500 men each; cohorts were divided into six centuries, each numbering some 80 men under the command of a junior officer, a centurion. The legion's smallest unit was the contubernia, a squad of about 8 men.

A typical legionary of the Roman army (far left) wore a sleeveless coat of iron mail over a woolen tunic. An iron helmet protected the soldier's head and face, and a large wooden shield — covered with leather and bound with iron — screened most of his body. Sturdy leather sandals with hobnailed soles half an inch thick allowed him to keep up a steady marching pace. His most formidable weapon was the pilum, a weighted throwing spear with a point sharp enough to penetrate armor, but in close combat he thrust with a short Spanish sword, or gladius.

A centurion (near left) wore silvered mail and leg armor called greaves, and he fought with a sword only. His chest amulet and decorative belt were insignia of rank.

Julius Caesar's campaign to subdue the Celtic tribes of Gaul reached a critical juncture in 52 BC when his army pinned down the forces of the rebel chief Vercingetorix at the stronghold of Alesia. Using a tactic employed by the Romans against Hannibal, Caesar encircled the enemy with siege works *(below)*, hoping to starve Vercingetorix into submission or provoke him to a reckless assault. The field facing the Gauls was sown with a fiendish array of hazards. Hidden beneath the brush were rows of barbed iron goads protruding from buried logs *(far left)*, and circular pits studded with sharp stakes; beyond lay a thicket of pointed branches, set at a menacing angle. Attackers who made it through the snares would have to cross two trenches — one of them filled with water diverted from a nearby river — then scale a steep wall while braving a barrage of missiles from the Romans in the towers. Aware that Vercingetorix had sent for a relief force to help break the siege, Caesar constructed an identical line of defenses facing outward. In time, the reinforcements arrived, and the Romans were assailed from both sides — but their works stood the test. As Caesar reported, the attackers "got themselves caught up on the goads, or they fell into the pits and impaled themselves, or else they were pierced and killed by the siege-spears that we hurled at them from the rampart and the towers." After a fierce effort, the Gauls fled in disarray, and Vercingetorix was taken prisoner, to be paraded in shackles through Rome's streets.

to the consulship. With the growth of the empire, however, a former praetor or consul could reasonably expect appointment as the governor of a province with virtually unlimited opportunities to feather his own nest.

Romans almost took it for granted that a governor would energetically plunder his province by accepting bribes, manipulating public contracts, selling supplies to the army, or applying any other personally rewarding corrupt practice. One favorite technique was to impose illegal taxes on the provincial peoples, buy the silence of administrative underlings by giving them a slice of the profits, then pocket the rest. During one year as a governor, the great orator Marcus Tullius Cicero made a considerable fortune — and he prided himself on his probity.

The problem, of course, was in climbing the ladder to the lofty and profitable perch of governor. At every rung the competition was cutthroat. Worse yet, the ascension to power was expensive: By the time a man became praetor, it was mandatory that he spend staggering sums of his own money to buy votes and woo the masses with public spectacles such as chariot races or gladiatorial contests. That meant ambitious politicians usually engaged in dubious practices from the outset, in order to accumulate the capital they needed to spend their way to higher office.

Within a few years after Sulla's leave-taking, three men emerged from the confusion to assert leadership roles. One was Gnaeus Pompeius, a soldier who had been so successful as one of Sulla's chief lieutenants that the dictator himself, who never completely trusted him, sarcastically bestowed upon him the name of Pompey the Great. Pompey later put down a rebellion in Spain, cleared the Mediterranean of pirates, pursued Mithradates of Pontus (who was causing trouble again) all the way to the Crimea, and conquered Syria and part of Palestine.

The second of the three leaders was Marcus Crassus, landowner, moneylender, speculator. Reputed to be Rome's richest citizen, he was so avaricious that even while

the dwellings of the city's poor were burning, as frequently occurred, Crassus sent slaves to purchase the properties at what were literally fire-sale prices. "No man is rich who cannot support an army," said Crassus, and it was his frustrated ambition to be a famed commander. He did earn the public's gratitude when he quelled a slave revolt led by an escaped gladiator named Spartacus. It was the nightmare Romans had long feared, an angry uprising by brutally treated agricultural slaves. Spartacus and his followers had defeated four Roman armies and had been at large for two years when Crassus suppressed the rebellion with savage cruelty, leaving the Appian Way lined with the crosses of some 6,000 crucified slaves.

The third was Julius Caesar, and he was immeasurably the greatest. Caesar had his faults. He was vain to the point of combing his hair forward and affecting a laurel wreath as a headpiece to conceal his baldness. Although a notorious rake, he divorced his second wife on the merest possibility of scandal, cynically explaining that "I demand of my wife that she must be above suspicion." And his vaulting ambition inspired fear in even his presumptive friends — who finally helped to do him in.

Yet in the sum of his many parts, Caesar loomed high above the rest. In a republic where every noble schoolboy practiced the arts of rhetoric, he was a spellbinding orator recognized even by the unfriendly Cicero as having a gift for stirring the "wretched starving mob." As an eminently lucid writer, he was a master at publicizing his own exploits. Perhaps most important, he was a brilliant military leader, Rome's greatest, unequalled in his understanding of army organization, from the fighting branches to commissary and engineering, and in his ability to win the loyalty of his men. And he was an astute politician who had moved steadily up the ladder of preferment before becoming a praetor in 62 BC.

As it happened, Pompey, Crassus, and Caesar all had grudges against the Senate's optimate oligarchy. Out of fear of the tremendous prestige Pompey had earned from his many victories, the Senate had refused to grant his army veterans the land allotments he had promised them. Crassus was angry because the Senate would not give financial relief to some followers of his, who had bid too much for the rights to collect Asian taxes. ("Tax farming," as such deals were called, was a common arrangement between government and private enterprise.) The Senate had also declined to grant him the major military command he so greatly desired. As for Caesar, who stemmed from an obscure patrician family, he had made a career out of championing the popularis cause, and he was vexed because the Senate was trying to undercut his campaign for a consulship.

It was, therefore, natural enough that the three should form a private coalition, later called the "First Triumvirate," to get Caesar elected consul and to pass legislation that would answer their individual purposes. They succeeded. Pompey's soldiers got their rewards, thereby ensuring their continued loyalty in whatever endeavor he might undertake. Crassus was eventually given an army, which he took to Parthia, where he predictably mangled a campaign and was killed in the process. Caesar, after serving as consul in 59 BC, was named governor of Cisalpine Gaul and the part of Transalpine Gaul where Rome held tenuous sway. There he would amass a fortune, largely by enslaving multitudes of barbarians who could be sold at profit, and win enduring military glory.

Hardly had Caesar assumed his new post when Helvetian tribesmen threatened his provincial territory with a mass migration from Switzerland. Caesar soon repulsed them — and kept on going. Indeed, he did not stop until, after nine years of almost constant fighting, he had stormed some 800 towns and conquered the whole of what later became France, along with parts of Switzerland and the Low Countries. Moreover, he launched expeditions against Britain that, although they fell short of conquest, opened the way for future operations.

Back in Rome, Pompey and the Senate by the late fifties BC at last found a commonality of interest: Both were envious of Caesar's successes and fearful of his ambitions. They determined together to put Caesar in his place. With Pompey's agreement, and in defiance of vetoes by the pro-Caesar tribunes, the Senate ordered Caesar to give up his command and come home for the good of the republic, or face charges of treason.

Upon receiving the news, Caesar knew that a return to Rome without his army probably would mean his death. He moved swiftly — and secretly. Under cover of darkness, he stole away from his headquarters in the Adriatic port city of Ravenna. Traveling southward in a carriage drawn by mules that had been borrowed from a

Standing by a round hut, a bareheaded Celt defends his home ground against a helmeted legionary in this Roman relief. Celtic resistance continued sporadically in Gaul even after the bitter defeat at Alesia, and Caesar responded with savage measures. After capturing the strategic hill fort of Uxellodunum in 50 BC, he cut off the hands of "all those who had carried weapons," one of his aides recounted, "so that everyone might see how evildoers were punished."

local baker, he arrived the next dawn at the Rubicon River, an otherwise insignificant stream that formed the boundary between Cisalpine Gaul and Roman Italy, where he was awaited by an advance guard of his legionaries. For a general heading for Rome to cross the Rubicon with troops was counted an act of treason. A time of fateful decision was at hand. Caesar hesitated only a moment. "We may still draw back," he said, "but once across that little bridge and the issue rests with the sword." Julius Caesar was nothing if not a gambler, and it was in a gambler's idiom that he declared his decision on that morning of January 11 in 49 BC. "The die is cast!" he cried, and with hoarse shouts his legionaries crossed the Rubicon. He entered Rome without resistance and seized the treasury. Learning of Caesar's reaction to the Senate edict, Pompey had withdrawn with his army to Greece, where Caesar pursued and defeated him. Pompey escaped and fled to Egypt, where he hoped to get some financial support from the wealthy boy-king Ptolemy XIII. Ptolemy, hoping to curry favor with Caesar, had Pompey stabbed to death as the Roman stepped from his ship. It is said that Caesar, who had pursued Pompey to Egypt, wept when Ptolemy later handed him his old ally's severed head.

Egypt — a very rich, quasi-independent country that was extremely important to anyone who wished to rule Rome — was torn by factional struggle. Caesar and his legions imposed order. Sometime during the fighting, the fifteen-year-old king disappeared, probably drowned. In his place Caesar set Ptolemy's sister (and wife), Cleopatra, who thus became the richest individual in the world.

Caesar soon went off to fight other wars, leaving Cleopatra pregnant with his son, who would be called Caesarion. On his return to Rome in 45 BC, he was awarded a triumphal celebration featuring a feast with 22,000 tables and was declared dictator by a submissive Senate. During his brief tenure he distributed land to some 80,000 Roman colonists, granted citizenship to Transalpine Gauls, opened the Senate to membership by some important provincial citizens, relieved debtors of some of the interest they owed, and introduced a new calendar. (This calendar would be used for the succeeding sixteen centuries, until some minor adjustments turned it into the modern Gregorian calendar).

But he also made his dictatorship permanent and assumed royal trappings, thus confirming the worst fears of the nobles who hoped to preserve the republic. And on the Ides of March 44 BC, sixty senatorial conspirators fell upon him as he presided over the assembly, inflicting twenty-three dagger wounds. Julius Caesar was dead.

News of Caesar's murder sped throughout the empire and to Apollonia, a Greek city on the Adriatic coast, where an eighteen-year-old named Gaius Octavius was completing his literary education. Gaius had every reason to be interested in the tidings: As Caesar's grandnephew, he had also been a protégé of the dictator, who had died without a legitimate son. Hastening back to Italy, Octavius was informed that the great Roman had left a will that made him Caesar's adopted son and heir. He also learned that there were two powerful citizens who considered themselves worthy successors to Caesar. One was Marcus Aemilius Lepidus, who had been the dictator's close friend and master of horse, which officially made him Caesar's second-in-command. Much more formidable was the handsome, swaggering Marcus Antonius (who would be remembered in the English-speaking world as Mark Antony). He had been Caesar's right-hand man and, although the position did not mean much under the dictatorship, was a consul at the time of the assassination.

The Celtic chiefs of southern Britain, who were first challenged by Julius Caesar in 55 BC and fell subject to Rome a century later, boasted a wealth of expertly crafted ornaments — including the ceremonial bronze shield at top, inlaid with red glass, and the braided gold torque below. This fine neck ring, found in the present-day English county of Norfolk, may have belonged to the ruling family of the Celtic tribe known as the Iceni. By one account, Queen Boudicca of the Iceni, who launched an ill-fated revolt against the Romans in AD 60, rode to battle wearing "a great twisted golden necklace."

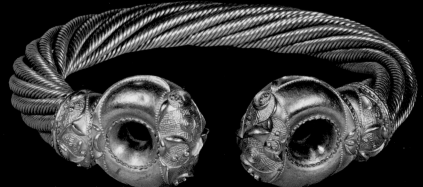

Mark Antony, Lepidus, and Octavius got along like scorpions in a bottle. Octavius took a new name, Gaius Julius Caesar, and won the support of veteran soldiers devastated by his granduncle's death. The Senate sided with him as well, largely on the notion that he would be amenable because of his youth and inexperience. "The boy is to be praised, honored, and elevated," said Cicero, making a double entendre with a Latin term that meant both "exalted" and "kicked upstairs."

For months, the rivals contended for supremacy before finally agreeing to a division of power. The Senate conferred on the Second Triumvirate a five-year term of autocratic power. The newly formed coalition immediately sought retribution against Caesar's assassins: Antony and Octavius hunted down Marcus Junius Brutus and Gaius Cassius Longinus, two of the leading tyrannicides, in Macedonia, and each of the murderers committed suicide after being defeated in a pair of battles fought at Philippi. Once that was done, the triumvirs turned on the Roman enemies they had accumulated over the years. By one account, some 300 senators and 2,000 equestrians were slain in the purge. At Mark Antony's insistence, one of the victims was Cicero, who had led Senatorial opposition to Antony. Cicero's head and hands were displayed nailed to the Rostra in the forum he had so often graced with his eloquence, one nail driven through the great orator's tongue.

Surprisingly, the triumvirs managed more or less to coexist until 36 BC, when Lepidus, who considered that he had got the short end of the division of power, attempted to capture Octavius in Sicily. But Lepidus's soldiers transferred their allegiance to Octavius because of his family connection to Caesar. Although Ledpidus's life was spared, he dwelt under armed guard for the rest of his days.

Antony, meanwhile, having been given control of Rome's eastern empire, had formed a strong political bond with Egypt's wealthy Queen Cleopatra that soon became a romantic one. In 40 BC he went back to Rome and entered into a political marriage with Octavius's sister, Octavia, but returned as soon as he could to Cleopatra's arms. His infidelity was an affront not only to Octavia but to Octavius, who was joined in his rage by nearly all of Rome when it was revealed that Antony was parceling out parts of the empire to Cleopatra and her children, including three he himself had sired.

At the urging of Octavius, the Roman Senate declared war on Antony, and Octavius himself accompanied the fleet that defeated the ships of Antony and Cleopatra in 31 BC at the Battle of Actium. Rather than be captured, the pair committed suicide, he by stabbing himself in the stomach, she by baring her arm to the fangs of an asp.

Sole power now was Octavius's for the asking. But when sycophants later suggested that he take over his adoptive father's role as dictator, he demurred with apparent dismay. Instead, he would accept — for life — the imperium that gave him Rome's supreme military command, and the power of a tribune. He would govern the empire as princeps, or "first citizen." And he would accept the name Augustus, the "revered one." It was by that felicitous name that he would rule during the decades that would become known as the golden age of the Roman Empire.

Outwardly, all the offices and institutions of the republic remained in place, and Augustus all his life would insist he had "restored the republic." The reality was different. True political power resided in the enigmatic man who adopted as his seal the symbol of the sphinx. As of 27 BC, when Augustus assumed his new authority, the republic was dead. Whatever his titles, an emperor now ruled the Roman Empire.

And Augustus proved an active imperialist indeed. To begin with, he pacified the territories Rome already held and made them secure by reforming their administration. He formally annexed Egypt, a vital source of grain for Rome. During his reign, the empire's north central border was pushed out to encompass what one day would be Austria and Hungary. (Fighting in Spain finally ended some two centuries after it had begun.) Augustus failed, however, in a plan to conquer Germany. The powerful and numerous peoples of that region remained free to threaten Rome in the future.

At home, Augustus continued to appoint senators to high-sounding positions. But for accomplishing day-to-day administrative work he relied upon the services of equestrians, freedmen, and slaves. As factotums of the imperial household, they were given deceptively innocuous titles — for example, the secretaries for correspondence and petitions were actually important state officials — and collectively they formed the beginnings of a Roman bureaucracy.

Augustus, a quintessential politician, was careful to court the masses. *Panem et circenses* — bread and circuses — were the cures for discontent, and he gave his subjects both in full measure. From the fertile lands of the empire poured the grains that were distributed free to the citizens of Rome. In his public entertainments, Augustus spared no expense. On one occasion, he staged a mock sea battle fought by a cast of 3,000 on an artificial lake.

Midway through his long regime, Augustus was named *Pontifex Maximus,* the head of Rome's state religion, and it is said that he was highly gratified by the appointment. Religion had suffered during the late republic. Augustus launched a movement to restore Rome's old gods to their former positions of importance and ordered the rehabilitation of eighty-two temples that had fallen into disrepair. He saw religion as a way to stimulate and focus patriotism, and it is likely that the massive building and rebuilding program Augustus undertook largely in the name of the gods was for purposes less than exclusively devotional.

He said that he found Rome a city of brick and turned it into one of marble. He was about half right; the city's poor still huddled in their brick insulae. Yet the emperor's accomplishments were undeniably awesome. In addition to the temples he restored, he constructed new ones that honored Mars, Venus, Apollo, and the newly deified Julius Caesar. Under his sponsorship Rome gained baths and basilicas, triumphal arches and porticoes, theaters and aqueducts. His prodigious program of public works had the practical effect of providing employment and spurring the economy.

As a literary man, Augustus himself possessed no great talents. His writing style was pleasant but unadorned. In his reading, he searched for passages that might be significant or useful to public service. These he filed and, when the occasion arose, dispatched to appropriate Roman officials. And yet it was perhaps the crowning splendor of Augustus's ca-

Among the legacies of Caesar Augustus to the city of Rome was the world's largest sundial, an ingenious device that used the shadow cast by an obelisk to indicate both hour and date. The idea had its genesis in the power struggle between the young Augustus — or Octavius, as he was then known — and Mark Antony. After informing a shocked public that Mark Antony had asked in his will to be buried in Egypt beside his beloved Cleopatra, Octavius shrewdly announced that he was erecting his own family crypt on the hallowed Field of Mars in Rome; the domed mausoleum *(background, left)* was completed shortly before he was named emperor in 27 BC. Later, Augustus used the same setting to remind his subjects that Egypt existed to serve Rome. He uprooted a sacred obelisk at Heliopolis, center of the Egyptian sun cult, and had it shipped to Rome to act as the gnomon, or shadow caster, for his sundial. The grid for the dial was marked out on a pavement of travertine. As diagramed at top, the tip of the obelisk's shadow moved from west to east as the day went on and from north to south as the months advanced — beginning with the winter solstice, under Capricorn, and ending with the summer solstice, under Cancer (for the remaining six months, the shadow lengthened, and so returned northward). The most significant day of the year for Augustus was the one he claimed as his birthday: September 23, or the fall equinox. Then, as on the spring equinox, the tip of the shadow moved east on a straight line. Capitalizing on that fact, Augustus built the Ara Pacis, or Temple of Peace, at the eastern end of the equinoctial line. Thus, as the sun set on the emperor's birthday, the shadow's point entered the temple, symbolizing Augustus's determination to be remembered as one "born for peace."

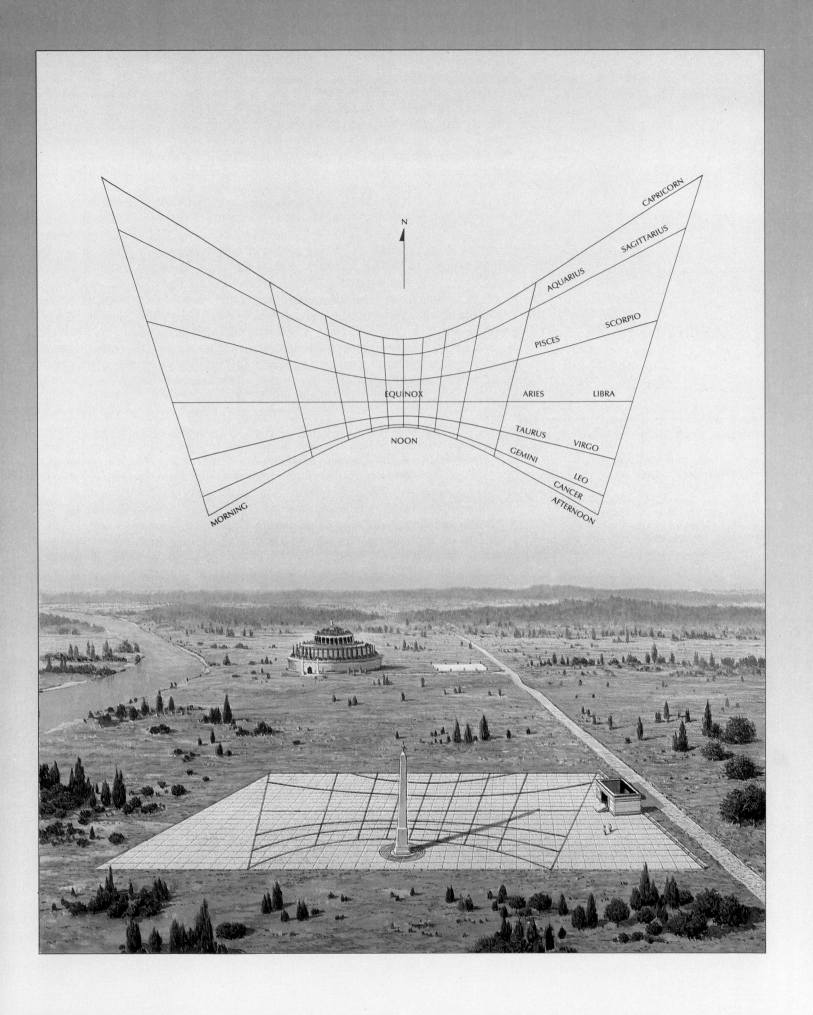

reer that under his sponsorship Latin literature flourished as it never had done before — and as it never would do again.

It had got off to a belated start in the late third century with the plays of Plautus and, a bit later, of Terence, both of whom modeled their work after the traditional comedies of the Greeks, right down to the stock character of the scheming slave. By the time Augustus was born, however, Roman poets had developed their own distinctive thrust. They were given to employing real people as characters in their work. For example, the Lesbia to whom Catullus addressed his elegant poems of love and disillusion was in fact a Roman lady named Clodia, who was probably the wife of a consul. Similarly, there could be no doubt that Julius Caesar and his chief of staff were the targets of Catullus's barbs — "each an equally avid adulterer, partners in competing for the girlies of the town." Caesar showed himself a pretty good sport about this. After demanding and getting an apology, he invited the poet to dinner.

Still, it remained for Augustus to offer official and invaluable sponsorship to the writers of his day. To assist him in that purpose, he used the wealthy Gaius Maecenas, one of his oldest and closest friends, in the role of talent scout. Maecenas drew into the imperial circle brilliant men from various levels of Roman society. The poets Ovid and Propertius were equestrians, the historian Livy came from a provincial family in Cisalpine Gaul, the great Virgil was the son of a small farmer, and Horace was born into a freedman's family.

To such men, the Augustan patronage meant social status and creature comforts at some cost to their intellectual freedom. Although Augustus did admit Livy to his family of friends, to the others he was mostly an aloof presence who patiently listened to their recitations. He generally refrained from censoring their works (one exception was Ovid, who was exiled because his eroticism offended Augustus), and he did not even require them to exalt his reign or himself — although many of them did anyway.

Augustus was certainly pleased when one of his protégés produced an epic poem for the greater glorification of Rome. Virgil was working on such a poem when he died in 19 BC. He had left orders that the work should be burned if he died without completing it. Augustus would have none of that — and the *Aeneid* was passed on to the world.

For the forty-five years of his reign, Augustus lived in a modest mansion atop the Palatine Hill, a small, retiring man who pulled the strings of the world's mightiest empire. Only in his final moment, in AD 14, did he allow a glimpse of what he may have been thinking all along. "Have I acted out the comedy well?" Augustus asked, and then he died.

The legacy of Augustus was an empire so strong that it survived for centuries the madness and monstrosities of many of his successors.

Augustus had adopted as his son his stepson and top general, Tiberius. At least nominally, Augustus had shared with Tiberius responsibility as his partner in the imperium and the Tribune's power. Tiberius seemed an apt choice. During long service in Gaul, Germany, Spain, and Armenia he had demonstrated real ability both as a soldier and an administrator.

By the time of his sponsor's death, however, Tiberius was nearly fifty-five years old and already a glum, deeply distrustful man who accepted the principate from a Senate that really had no other choice. Tiberius made lethal use of the so-called *lex maiestatis*, "the law of grandeur," to do away with enemies both real and imagined. The catchall law, which forbade behavior that might "diminish the majesty of the Roman people,"

Some early Roman emperors may have taken on divine airs, but they were men of mere mortal capacities, prone to the same passions and woes that beset their subjects. A sense of the raw humanity of the rulers and their wives is conveyed by their portraits, works designed to reveal force of character. To be sure, artistic concessions might be made to vanity. Caligula was so ashamed of his baldness that he forbade anyone to look on him from above, and sculptors portrayed him with a full head of hair *(page 80)*. Other rulers were less fastidious, as the unflattering bust of Vespasian shows *(page 82)*. Such sculptural realism had its literary counterpart in the essays of the biographer Suetonius, who probed the feats and foibles of the caesars with clinical skill. He may have exaggerated certain emperors' vices, but his work exemplifies the willingness of Roman artists to explore the harsh features of their subjects.

PORTRAITS OF THE POWERFUL

A leader of great cunning, Augustus enacted measures to discourage adultery while pursuing his own romantic urges, as

Augustus's union with Livia was childless, so at his death power passed to Livia's son by a previous marriage, Tiberius, the first ruler of the Claudian line. As suggested by these portraits, the offshoots of this proud stock were a sullen lot, who regarded those around them with suspicion, if not outright hostility. According to Suetonius, the aging Tiberius accepted the sadistic behavior of his grandnephew and heir apparent, Caligula *(far left)*, with cynical fatalism: "I am nursing a viper for the Roman people." Caligula made good that prediction with a ven-omous reign that saw many a citizen killed in the torturous manner demanded by the emperor: "Make him feel that he is dying!" After Caligula's assassination, the scholarly Claudius *(below)* took the throne. His reign was temperate until he fell under the influence of his niece, the widow Agrippina *(left)*, who "had a niece's privilege of kissing and caressing Claudius, and exercised it with a noticeable effect on his passions." After their marriage, Claudius adopted Agrippina's son Nero *(lower left)*, whose evil legend would ultimately eclipse even Caligula's.

Vespasian, the emperor who delivered Rome from the chaos that followed Nero's death, was free of the vanity that consumed his predecessors. He restored stability at home, Suetonius related, by renouncing purges: "No innocent party was ever punished . . . except behind his back." Vespasian dealt ruthlessly with opponents abroad, however, crushing a revolt of the Jews with the help of his son Titus.

Coming to power some twenty years after Vespasian, Trajan followed in his predecessor's path by avoiding palace intrigue and concentrating on conquest. Leading his troops across the Danube, he inflicted such a devastating defeat on the Dacians that their domain would come to be known by its conquerors' name — Romania.

Trajan's handpicked successor, the judicious Hadrian, was so enamored of Greek culture that he affected the beard and curled hair of Hellenic heroes. His fondest companion was a youth named Antinous, who drowned as the two were voyaging up the Nile in AD 130 and was subsequently worshiped around the eastern Mediterranean as a martyr of sorts.

ultimately carried the death penalty for anyone found guilty of so much as murmuring unkind words about the emperor.

Tiberius retired during the last decade of his life to the beautiful isle of Capri, leaving a right-hand man, Sejanus, to manage affairs in Rome. Sejanus's excesses in pursuit of ambition helped make Tiberius unpopular. Upon the death of Tiberius at age seventy-eight, exulting mobs flocked in Rome's streets. Although the old emperor could not conceivably have realized it, the most significant event of his reign had been the crucifixion in faraway Jerusalem of a man named Jesus, of Nazareth.

Rome's rejoicing was premature. Tiberius's offenses could not compare with those attributed to his grandnephew and successor, Caligula (as he would be called by posterity, although his real name was Gaius Caesar and he actually detested the nickname, which meant "Bootkins"; it was bestowed upon him by legionaries to whom he had been a sort of mascot during his childhood). "Remember," Caligula once said, "that I can do anything to anybody" — and he did. Although his own sister Drusilla was married to a former consul, it was rumored that Caligula abducted her and made her his mistress. Upon her death, he decreed days and weeks of public mourning on which Romans were forbidden to bathe or laugh. Taking pleasure in witnessing the torture of condemned men, he allegedly once enjoyed counting off all the prisoners "between the first bald head and the last" — and ordering them thrown to wild beasts for entertainment. Demanding that his favorite horse be named a consul, he rigged the animal out in blankets of royal purple.

Determining to conquer Britain, he assembled his legions on the continental shores of the channel. Unfortunately, he had neglected to provide ships, whereupon he set the soldiers to gathering sea shells. Worst of all, having spent his inherited fortune, he began to levy absurdly confiscatory taxes.

Finally, his own Praetorian Guard — the elite force originally established by Augustus to protect the person of the emperor — could stand it no longer. In AD 41, after almost four years of the mad emperor, several of the guards set upon Caligula, left him dying of thirty sword and dagger wounds, murdered his wife, and smashed his little girl's head against a wall.

Later, while the Senate was longwindedly debating the possibility of restoring the republic, the Praetorian Guards took the matter of imperial succession into their own hands. Searching through the palace for a possible candidate, guardsmen found Caligula's fifty-year-old uncle hiding behind a curtain in mortal fear that he was next in line for assassination. Instead, the guards acclaimed him as emperor and forced their choice upon the Senate.

His name was Claudius, and his performance as emperor was a surprise to many. He had been constitutionally weak since birth, and although the specific nature of his debilities is unknown, they were such that his own mother, asserting that nature had "only begun, not completed" Claudius, described him as "a monster." For that matter, his stepgrandfather, the great Augustus, had required that he be kept out of public view "lest he should do something that could be seen and laughed at."

Thus sequestered, Claudius had turned to scholarship, interesting himself in philology and phonetics and authoring a prodigious number of histories, including one work of forty-one volumes.

Installed as emperor, Claudius gathered about himself a number of remarkably able freedmen who acted as a sort of general staff in charge of an administrative apparatus that was considerably advanced from the embryonic civil service set up by Augustus.

Looking abroad, Claudius determined to push ahead with the project so tentatively started by Caesar — the conquest of Britain. After a textbook campaign, in which Claudius briefly led the army before leaving the rest to his generals and returning to Rome, Britain was declared a province, although fighting would be necessary for generations to come.

During his brief time in supreme power, Julius Caesar had moved toward granting the Roman franchise to highly placed men of certain provinces. Augustus disagreed and drew back, but Claudius went even further, among other things making it possible for Gallic chieftains to become members of the Roman Senate.

In so doing, Claudius took a significant step along the course that in a later century would inspire a visiting professor from Asia Minor to wax eloquent to Romans on what he considered to be their empire's greatest accomplishment: "I mean your magnificent citizenship with its grand conception." There was, he said, "nothing like it in the records of all mankind. . . . You have everywhere appointed to your citizenship, and even to kinship with you, the better part of the world's talent, courage, and leadership."

But whatever his merits, Claudius was both unwise and singularly unfortunate in his choice of wives, of whom he had four. The last and most ambitious was his own niece, Julia Agrippina, a virago with a son by a previous marriage whose name was Nero. Obsessed with advancing Nero's interests, Agrippina bullied her husband first into adopting the boy and then into moving him ahead of the emperor's own son, Britannicus, in the line of imperial succession.

With those preliminaries out of the way, Agrippina allegedly placed before Claudius a generous helping of one of his favorite dishes — mushrooms — which the old man devoured with great gusto. The mushrooms turned out to be poisonous, and Claudius perished shortly thereafter.

Ascending to the throne, the seventeen-year-old Nero soon set the style for his murderous reign. He started out his rule by poisoning his stepbrother and potential rival, Britannicus. Later on, when his domineering mother got to be bothersome, he had her assassinated.

Fancying himself not only a patron but a performer of the arts, Nero shocked Rome by appearing on stage to sing and play a lyre. For the nobility, attendance was mandatory, and, wrote the historian Suetonius, "no one was allowed to leave the theater even for the most urgent reasons. And so it is said that some women gave birth to children there."

In AD 64, much of Rome was consumed by a catastrophic fire that raged for nearly a week. As described by Tacitus, "The blaze in its fury ran first through the lower portions of the city, rose to the hills, then again devastated the lower portions." Rome's ashes were still smoldering when rumors swept the city that the emperor had himself set the fire, then watched it while strumming his lyre and singing of the destruction of ancient Troy.

In fact, Nero had been at Antium, about thirty-five miles away, when the fire broke out, and upon his return he promptly placed the blame on Christians, who had by then appeared in Rome in considerable numbers. Although they were no threat whatever to Nero's regime, they did make convenient scapegoats. Terrible persecutions followed the fire, and on at least one occasion Christians were tarred, staked, and torched to provide illumination in the emperor's garden.

Beyond that, Nero used the fire as an excuse to rebuild Rome according to his own

Even as the Roman caesars strengthened their hold upon the ancient world and were elevated to a status bordering on the divine, a new faith was born — a religion that would long outlive the power and glory of Imperial Rome.

At the age of 30, Jesus of Nazareth, a Jewish carpenter from the province of Galilee in Palestine, set out on the brief but remarkable mission that would give birth to the Christian religion. Rejecting both the pantheistic theology of Rome and the stricter of Judaism's doctrines, Jesus preached that eternal life was accessible to everyone and that virtue and repentance would win such salvation. His charismatic personality, the simple but eloquent nature of his philosophy, and his renown as a healer of the sick and infirm, convinced a number of Jews that Jesus was their long awaited Messiah, or Christ — a word of Greek derivation meaning the "anointed one."

Although Jesus won many followers, his teachings also aroused a great deal of fear and hatred. Some important Jewish leaders were appalled by his disregard of traditional religious law, while Roman authorities came to regard him as a dangerous revolutionary. After three years of proselytizing, Jesus was arrested in Jerusalem, put on trial and condemned by Jewish and Roman courts, then crucified.

Soon after Jesus' execution, his closest disciples claimed to have witnessed his miraculous resurrection, confirming that he was indeed the Messiah. They continued his work, and eventually their experiences and beliefs were chronicled in the four gospels of the New Testament. By far the most important of the early Christian missionaries was Paul, a former Jewish official from Tarsus in Asia Minor. In the course of his travels through Syria, Cyprus, Asia Minor, and Greece, Paul preached to and converted thousands of men and women and was widely regarded as Christianity's most eloquent and persuasive spokesman.

Although he paid for his beliefs with his life, Paul helped to plant the seeds of Christianity in Rome. Initially, most Romans believed Christianity to be a Jewish mystery cult and Jesus a mere magician, undeserving of recognition as divine. The fact that the majority of Jews refused to acknowledge the new Messiah seemed to confirm that the Christian faith was, as the historian Tacitus observed, "a baneful superstition." But as the numbers of Christians increased, their open rejection of pagan beliefs and their denial of imperial divinity appeared to many Romans to threaten the stability of the empire. The first large-scale persecution of Christians occurred in the city of Rome during the reign of the emperor Nero in AD 64, and other purges followed. But in the end the new faith would triumph — eventually to become the state religion of Rome itself.

A NEW FAITH

A fragment from a Roman tombstone bears some of the earliest examples of Christian symbols. A cruciform anchor represents hope, while two fish evoke Jesus' words to his disciples, "I will make you fishers of men."

tastes, and his mammoth construction program very nearly bankrupted the government. By that time, it was rumored Nero was planning to recall and execute several provincial governors, which led commanders in Gaul, Africa, and Spain to launch a series of preemptive revolts. When the Praetorian Guard also declared its hostility, Nero panicked, fled the city, and as his enemies closed in on him, took his own life.

He left behind him an empire in chaos. During the incredible next year of AD 69, no fewer than four men in turn accepted the scepter of the Roman imperium. Each of the four was a provincial commander or governor; each was acclaimed and elevated by soldiers loyal to his cause. Two were murdered, and one died a suicide. Yet from the bloodbath there arose a survivor who would rule for a decade and who would lead the empire out of what a historian of that era would call, with considerable restraint, "a period rich in disaster."

The successful emperor was a distinguished old soldier named Vespasian. Vespasian had been putting down a serious rebellion in Judea when word came that the imperial throne was vacant. Gathering support from Roman legions in Syria and North Africa, he marched back to Rome, where the Senate confirmed his rule. His son Titus finished the job of quelling the Judean revolt, in the process destroying Jerusalem in AD 70 and capturing the stronghold of Masada in AD 73, as its Jewish defenders committed mass suicide.

Vespasian managed to put the empire back on a sound financial basis mainly by pinching pennies and increasing taxes — including a levy on the urine used in fulling cloth. Although such measures were naturally unpopular, Vespasian saw his duty, did it, and died with a smile on his lips. "Dear me!" he said as he felt his life slipping away. "I think I am turning into a god."

Vespasian was followed by his son Titus, an enormously popular young man — "the love and darling of mankind," said one Roman — who took a fever and died within two years of his accession. He was succeeded by his brother Domitian who would, during the fifteen years of his regime, fully earn the scathing description of the satirist Juvenal as a "bald Nero." A sadist who enjoyed nothing more than impaling flies on a stylus, he suffered a paranoid fear for his own life, and his pervasive network of informers was the terror of Rome. Finally his fears were fulfilled, and he was stabbed to death by a household servant.

By the time of Domitian's demise it must surely have seemed that Rome's ship of state was in dangerous waters and perhaps in peril of foundering. And yet, astoundingly, it was about to enter the long and prosperous period that would eventually become known as the era of "the five good emperors."

The first was Nerva, a respectable old gentleman who was elected by his senatorial peers and died a little more than a year afterward. Before he died, however, the army forced him to adopt as his son and to groom as his successor a man chosen on the basis of military ability.

The choice was a good one. The new emperor, Trajan, was born in Spain of Italian stock. He had built a solid record as a commander in Syria and Spain. Under his imperium, the boundaries of empire achieved their farthest reach as Ro-

Attended by a winged Victory, the bearded Marcus Aurelius parades into Rome through a triumphal arch. This most reflective of emperors was compelled to spend much of his reign in the field, defending the empire's northern and western borders. Although he accepted popular acclaim, he remained skeptical of such pomp, advising all those who earned laurels to strive for detachment: "Ponder the life led by others long ago, the life that will be led after you, the life being led in uncivilized races; how many do not even know your name, how many will very soon forget it, and how many, who praise you perhaps now, will very soon blame you."

man legions marched across the Danube into Dacia and, later, into Armenia and Parthian-ruled Mesopotamia. (In the end, Mesopotamia proved impossible to hold.) The son of a colonial family, Trajan knew the problems of provincial cities where local officials had been allowed a generally free hand, all too often to their own enrichment. Trajan tightened the reins by sending Roman curators to supervise the municipalities.

So much was predictable. Far more surprisingly, the rough old soldier launched a massive program of public assistance to the poor. Setting aside the equivalent of a year's imperial budget, the emperor used it to found a system of farm loans at low rates. The interest income, in turn, was directed to the support of orphans and the children of poor families.

In the same way as Nerva had done for him, Trajan in turn trained his own successor, taking as ward his young kinsman Hadrian. Although Hadrian, like Trajan, proved to be a brilliant general, he was to a much greater degree than his predecessor had been an intellectual citizen of the cosmopolitan world that the Roman Empire had become. Tutored in Greek as a boy, he remained devoted throughout his life to Hellenistic art and Platonic philosophy.

Upon becoming emperor after the death of Trajan in AD 117, Hadrian recognized that Trajan's expansionism was threatening the stability of the empire. He therefore gave up some of Trajan's territorial acquisitions, drew in his lines from their exposed positions, and went on the defensive. He built along the German frontier a line of fortifications that extended for 200 miles, all the way from the Rhine to the Danube; and in Britain he constructed a seventy-three-mile-long wall to protect the Roman south from the unconquered north.

Hadrian traveled tirelessly, a frequent presence in Greece and Gaul and Germany, in Egypt and Asia Minor. By the time of his death in AD 138, Rome for the first time in its history was perhaps more respected than feared, and its prestige was by no means diminished during the reigns of his successors, the peace-loving Antoninus Pius and the philosophical Marcus Aurelius, who ruled until AD 180. By this time, the empire was experiencing some difficulties that would become increasingly significant. Economic problems were evident. Beyond the northern frontiers, barbarians were acquiring greater military and political sophistication. And major plagues carried home from the East by Roman soldiers were eating into imperial manpower. Before long, Augustus's empire would be seriously threatened.

THE MASTER BUILDERS

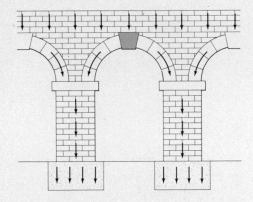

The Romans possessed an unrivaled talent for engineering — a point conceded even by the Greeks, whose own architectural accomplishments were considerable. The Greek geographer and historian Strabo, who visited Rome early in the first century AD, observed that the city's engineers excelled in areas "neglected by the Greeks, such as the construction of roads and aqueducts, and of sewers that could wash the filth of the city into the Tiber. They have built paved roads throughout the country, leveling ridges and filling up hollows, so as to make possible the movements of heavily loaded wagons. . . . And such is the quantity of water brought in by the aqueducts, that veritable rivers flow through the city and its sewers: almost every house has cisterns, waterpipes, and copious fountains."

The roads and aqueducts were the arteries of Rome. But its vital organs were the great public halls: spacious heated baths to cleanse the citizens, vast arenas to amuse them, soaring temples to glorify their heavenly and earthly masters. Wherever the Romans ventured in their campaigns, they brought with them this passion for city building. Troops laid down roads through the wilderness, and their camps became permanent settlements; aqueducts nurtured the growth of the towns, and public buildings rose. Once installed in imposing quarters, the Romans proceeded to draw the people of the surrounding territory into their civic web.

All this was accomplished through the systematic application of a few simple engineering principles. The graceful strength of the arch, a form bequeathed to the Romans by the Etruscans, was deftly exploited to carry heavy aqueducts over rivers and valleys. And knowledge of the arch led to the vault — a broad enclosure that could reach massive proportions without internal pillars. The Romans worked wonders as well with a few basic building materials. Although the terrain around Rome offered little hard stone that could be easily quarried, it was rich in a volcanic sand known as pozzolana. Mixed with lime and water, this substance yielded a cement that would set even below the surface of rivers and bays. In time, Roman engineers learned to blend the cement with various aggregates to make concrete. Strong and seamless, molded concrete proved the perfect medium for the grand designs of the city builders.

The final ingredient in the Roman formula for engineering success was as old as the pyramids of Egypt — the ability to organize masses of unskilled laborers into an efficient work force. The good builder had to be both a technician and an overseer, as Nonius Datus, a Roman engineer of the second century AD, learned to his chagrin. Assigned to tunnel through a hill for an aqueduct to the North African city of Saldae, he carefully surveyed the site, drew his plans, and supervised the breaking of ground on either side of the hill before being called away. Returning a few years later, he found that the two digging crews, assigned to meet halfway, had each veered slightly to their right. "Had I waited a little longer before coming," the engineer wrote after remedying the situation, "Saldae would have possessed two tunnels instead of one!"

Standing on its own, the arch was a vivid symbol of Roman might, a triumphal gateway for victorious generals and a yoke for their defeated enemies. The Arch of Titus *(left),* built to commemorate the emperor's subjugation of the rebellious Judaeans in AD 70, was crowned by a gilded image of Titus in his chariot. Beneath the sculpture lay a dedication to Titus and carved reliefs celebrating his prowess — including a view of Titus's troops carrying sacred treasures taken from the Temple at Jerusalem.

Free-standing arches needed massive piers to absorb the weight pressing outward along the curve from the center. When arches were strung together, however, the stress on the piers was lessened, and they could be built more economically. As shown below, the outward thrust from adjoining arches was resolved vertically in the intervening pier, and the load was transferred safely to the foundation.

The most delicate sequence in the construction of an arch came after the foundation was laid and the piers raised. Using the projecting imposts atop the pier for support, the builders set up a temporary semicircular timber frame. Above it they arranged precisely chiseled blocks, or voussoirs, wedging in a large keystone at the center to lock the pieces in place.

ANATOMY OF THE ARCH

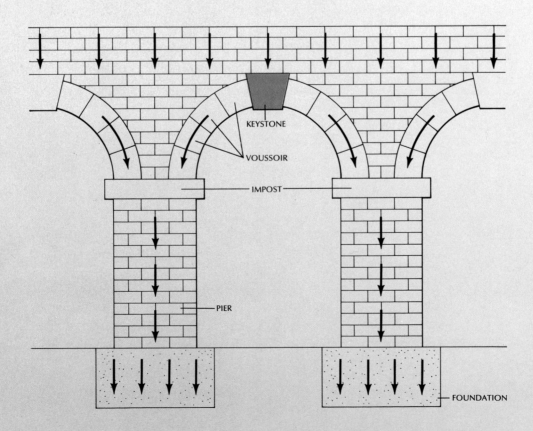

KEYSTONE

VOUSSOIR

IMPOST

PIER

FOUNDATION

Around AD 120, the emperor Hadrian, a cultivated man with a passion for architecture, commissioned a building that would stand as a monument to the highest aspirations of imperial Rome. Known as the Pantheon, or the place of all gods, the structure was a roofed rotunda ringed with seven recesses that may have been designed as shrines for the deities the Romans associated with the heavens — including Mars, Mercury, Venus, and Jupiter. The dome capping the hall was envisioned as a symbol of the firmament. Through its open eye, or oculus, the sun's rays could penetrate to gild the marble floor below even as Hadrian held court.

Providing support for the weight of such a vast canopy was a monumental challenge for the engineers. They began by laying a sturdy subterranean foundation — a ring of concrete fifteen feet deep and twenty-four feet wide. On this circle they raised eight concrete piers spaced to create the seven recesses. Each massive pier was artfully disguised as a temple front, with fluted columns and a pedestal for statuary.

The dome itself was the most demanding part of the project. Atop scaffolding, workers constructed a wooden mold, as they had below, to receive the concrete. The dome was coffered to reduce weight and buttressed on the outside in stairstep fashion. As work progressed upward, finer grades of concrete were applied; at the highest rung, the mixers blended their cement with pumice, one of the lightest of stones.

So sound were the builders' methods and materials that the Pantheon would endure long after other ancient monuments crumbled. Within a few centuries of Hadrian's death, Christian martyrs replaced pagan deities as objects of veneration, but the sanctuary lost none of its character. Nearly 1,700 years after its construction, the English poet Percy Bysshe Shelley would stand in the hall and wonder at "the perfection of its proportions," likening the canopy above to "the unmeasured dome of Heaven."

A HEAVENLY DOME

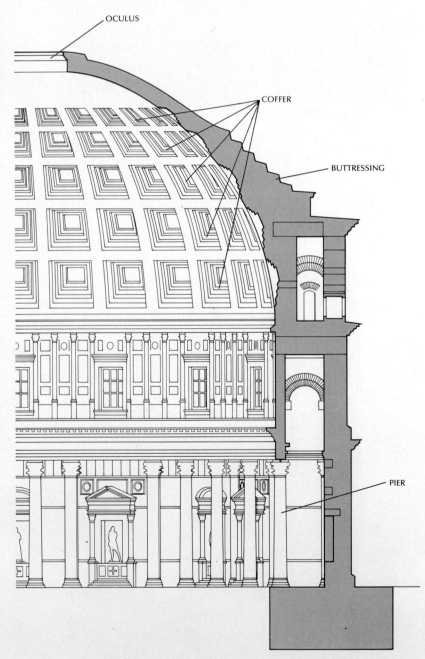

OCULUS

COFFER

BUTTRESSING

PIER

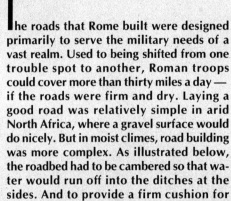

ROADS FOR THE EMPIRE

The roads that Rome built were designed primarily to serve the military needs of a vast realm. Used to being shifted from one trouble spot to another, Roman troops could cover more than thirty miles a day — if the roads were firm and dry. Laying a good road was relatively simple in arid North Africa, where a gravel surface would do nicely. But in moist climes, road building was more complex. As illustrated below, the roadbed had to be cambered so that water would run off into the ditches at the sides. And to provide a firm cushion for heavy loads, the foundation was composed of compact layers. Typically, sand was deposited at the bottom of the ditch and rolled flat. Small stones made up the second layer, gravel the third, and paving stones were laid on top. An ancient historian noted that the Roman consul Appius Claudius Crassus, who built the Appian Way *(left)* from Rome to Capua around 300 BC, "caused all the paving stones to be polished and cut so as to form angles and had them jointed together without any kind of cement. They adhered so strongly that to look at them they do not seem to be jointed at all but to form one whole mosaic of stone." Over the years, this durable surface carried not only troops and their supply wagons but merchants' carts and postal carriages.

Like other Roman engineering feats, road building was a grueling business that required a disciplined work force. The troops did most of the spadework — an arrangement that kept them fit and out of mischief between campaigns, although on rare occasions the soldiers rebelled. At times the burden was foisted off on subject peoples, such as the Caledonians of Britain. In AD 86 the Caledonian chief Calgacus led an unsuccessful revolt, protesting that "the Romans consume our hands and bodies in making roads through woods and marshes."

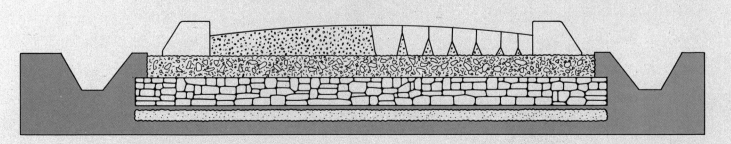

The Roman world was organized around cities, and where cities did not exist they had to be created — a project that required an abundant supply of fresh water. When Roman officials in Gaul arrived at the raw settlement of Nemausus, or present-day Nîmes, to lay out an administrative center there, they found a fine spring at the site that would have met the needs of a modest population. But the plans for Nemausus were far from modest, and around 20 BC the gifted administrator Marcus Agrippa began construction of a thirty-one-mile-long aqueduct to supply the fledgling town. Like the famous aqueducts of Rome, the watercourse would operate by force of gravity: Originating at a copious spring in the hills northeast of Nemausus, it would descend ever so gradually to its destination. Standing in the way was the gorge of the Gardon River — 180 feet deep, or more than twice the extent of the tallest arch the Romans could construct without risking a collapse. Agrippa responded by spanning the ravine with a triple-tiered structure that would be known to posterity as the Pont du Gard, or Bridge of the Gard *(right)*. The lowest tier was built wide enough to carry both a paved road and the piers supporting the heavy cement conduit, encased in masonry atop the bridge.

Once the aqueduct was completed, officials needed a way to manage the flow. Even if the supply of water from the source remained constant, leaks were sure to develop along the aqueduct through wear and tear or through subterfuge. (Resourceful property owners were known to tap into the conduit.) To cope with reductions, an ingenious sluice like the one diagrammed opposite was installed outside Nemausus.

The success of this versatile water-supply system can be gauged by the rapid growth of Nemausus. Within decades, temples and arenas, houses and baths were sprouting up there. Another city in the image of Rome was emerging.

THE LIFELINES OF ROME

To distribute water from an aqueduct, Roman engineers used a sluice with channels.

When the flow was reduced by drought or leaks, barriers blocked the side channels *(near right)*, and the supply moved through the central passage to communal fountains. A moderate flow *(center)* meant that the water would crest the lower of the side barriers, and public conveniences such as baths would be supplied as well.

A heavy flow *(far right)* filled all channels, providing water to homes.

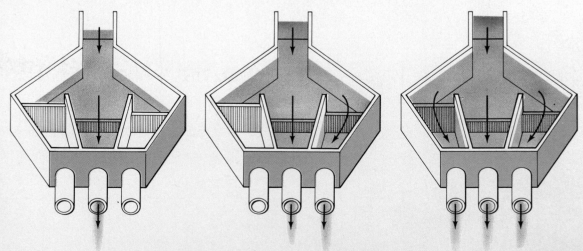

For all their monumental undertakings, the Romans seldom lost sight of the need for sheer comfort in the places they designed. This quest for contentment was exemplified by one Gaius Sergius Orata, whose contribution to the ease of his fellow citizens grew, oddly enough, out of his commercial interest in harvesting seafood. Around 80 BC, Orata hit on an idea for cultivating oysters year-round in the warm waters known to promote their growth.

He elevated a series of tanks on brick pillars, enclosed them at the base, and installed furnaces to circulate hot air beneath the tanks. Before long, Orata was applying the same principle to human habitats. Buying up neglected villas, he equipped them with heated baths and with flues that warmed entire rooms, then resold the homes at a tidy profit. Although few Romans could afford such

THE COMFORT OF THE BATHS

residences, citizens throughout the empire were soon basking in the glow of central heating as similar systems were installed in public baths, including the one at Pompeii illustrated here.

The heat for the Pompeii bath emanated from a furnace (below), stoked most likely by slaves. A boiler fed hot water into the bath, while warm air from the fire beneath the tank rose through the hollow walls and warmed the room. This cozy chamber, known as the *caldarium,* adjoined another bathing room, the *tepidarium,* which was kept lukewarm. Beyond lay the *frigidarium,* where hardy citizens, having taken their ease in the heated compartments, could brace themselves for renewed activity with a quick cold dip.

For the many who visited the complex regularly, the bath was a source of civic pride — a marvel of technology that afforded the common citizen imperial pleasures.

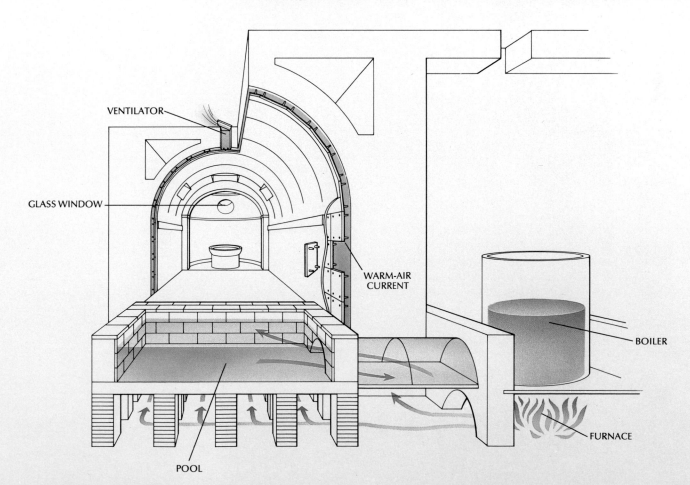

VENTILATOR

GLASS WINDOW

WARM-AIR CURRENT

BOILER

FURNACE

POOL

THE QUEST FOR POWER IN THE EAST

3 The invasion of India by Alexander the Great revealed a new and astonishing world to Europeans. The Greeks in his army, and those who followed later to the subcontinent, returned with breathless descriptions of Indian wonders that left their audiences open-mouthed. One who reported about this amazing land was Megasthenes, a Greek historian and diplomat who apparently spent some time in India around the end of the fourth century BC as the envoy of a Seleucid king. So riveting were Megasthenes' accounts that other Greek and Roman writers tirelessly quoted what he had to say.

From such sources came descriptions of twelve-foot-long freshwater fish that Indians caught with their bare hands in the shallow waters of receding floods, of shrimp that grew larger than crabs, and of fox-sized ants that turned up gold dust as they burrowed into the earth. (The gold was left for the taking by anyone brave enough to risk being pursued and killed by the ferocious ants.) There were tales of twenty-four-foot-long snakes that could swallow stags whole, of elephants that danced and played cymbals attached to their forelegs, of birds that could "be taught to speak, as children are taught." And high in the mountains of the Indian frontier, it was said, lived "a peculiar kind of animal shaped like a satyr, covered all over with shaggy hair." These beasts were able to "dart up the precipices with incredible speed" and "defend themselves by rolling down stones on their assailants" — all attributes indicating that this may have been one of the earliest reports of the yeti, the fabled abominable snowman of the Himalayas.

There was no way for a reader or listener in the Hellenistic world, even a skeptical one, to sort out truth from falsehood in such descriptions of India, since some of the actual facts were at least as startling as the myths with which they were intertwined: Greeks back home probably were as surprised to learn that birds called parrots could be taught to speak, for instance, as they were to hear that ants the size of foxes worked at mining gold. People in Greece, who knew nothing of cotton or sugarcane, were filled with wonder at tales of "trees on which wool grows" and a "miraculous reed" that yielded honey without the intervention of bees. The agricultural abundance of India, in fact, may well have been the most astonishing fact of all to those who dwelled in the dry region around the Aegean.

This immense land, wrote Megasthenes, which seemed "well-nigh to embrace the whole of the northern tropic zone of the earth," abounded in "fruit trees of every kind and many vast plains of great fertility." Famine had never visited India, he reported inaccurately, "since there is a double rainfall in the course of each year — one in the winter season, when the sowing of wheat takes place and the second at the time of the summer solstice, which is the proper season for sowing rice as well as sesame and millet. The inhabitants almost always gather two harvests annually; and even should one prove abortive, they are always sure of the other crop." India's natural treasures extended underground as well, reported Megasthenes, ''for the soil contains much gold and silver and copper and iron in no small quantity, and even tin and other metals, which are employed in making articles of use and ornament and accouterments of war.''

Such was the exotic earthly paradise that greeted Alexander — and shortly bade him farewell. The great warrior was able to claim only a small corner of the vast land for his empire before being forced to turn back by his disgruntled troops. Most of India remained, for the moment, a fragmented collection of self-governing, sometimes-warring kingdoms and republics and smaller tribal communities, some of them fabulously rich and culturally advanced. But although Alexander was unable to weld India into an empire, that land had already spawned its own man of vision and ambition who before long was to found an indigenous Indian imperial government and bestow upon the people of the subcontinent the benefits of unity.

This leader was Chandragupta Maurya, a man whose ancestry and early years are clouded in mystery. His surname, Maurya, probably derived from the word for peacock, perhaps in reference to some ancient totem of his clan. Some said he was sired

As Alexander the Great's far-flung domain disintegrated after his death, two other empires emerged in Asia. A former subject of Alexander's, Chandragupta Maurya, united the warring kingdoms of northwestern India and founded the Mauryan dynasty. His successors, most notably the charismatic Asoka, extended the Mauryan empire throughout the Indian subcontinent. In Persia, the warlike Parthians conquered the remnants of Alexander's Seleucid empire to become the dominant power in the region. Although the western portion of their empire was at times occupied by Roman forces (orange area on map), Parthian armies successfully defended the bulk of their empire against invading Roman legions and ensured control of the vital trade routes to the east.

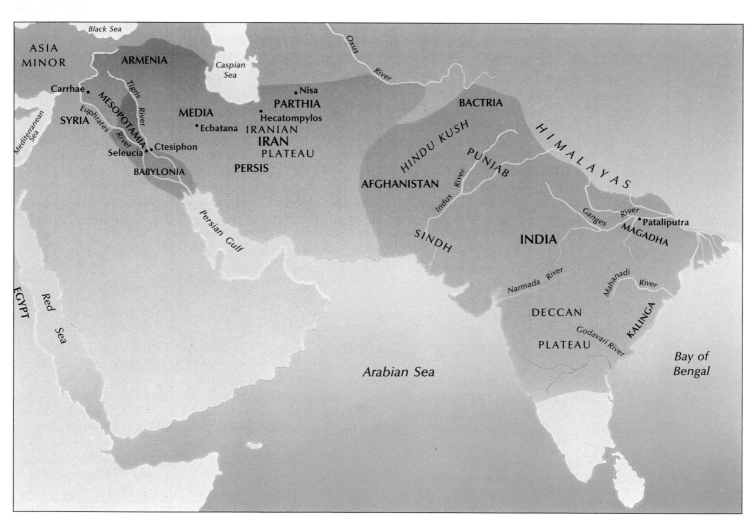

by a common herdsman, others that he was a prince of the Moriya tribe who had fled into exile when a larger kingdom took over his own small state. He apparently met Alexander while the conqueror was in India, but Alexander's chroniclers dismissed him as a "young stripling" and gave him little further notice.

Whatever his birth, this stripling was destined to become India's first emperor. With the aid of a high-caste Hindu Brahman advisor named Kautilya, he would found a Mauryan succession of rulers who would not only bring to the Indian subcontinent the concept of empire but would suffuse government with new ideals — of rule by law, of the duties as well as the privileges of absolute monarchs, of the responsibilities of the powerful in matters of spiritual growth and public welfare.

In this same era, another empire would come into being in a neighboring but very different region, the Iranian plateau, to the west across the Hindu Kush mountains from India. Here, in a windblown and desiccated land, a restless horde of horsemen called Parthians would be propelled on an epic course of conquest by a chieftain named Arsaces. The dynasty that ruled this brawling, erratic people would survive for about half a millennium, almost three times as long as the idealistic Mauryans. It would take its subjects from poverty to riches and back again, would hack away all but a few remnants of the last Greek holdings in Asia, and, on more than one occasion, would humble Rome's mighty legions at the zenith of their power. And just as India gave Europeans a look at one unfamiliar and intriguing world, so the Parthian empire, because of its strategic position where trade routes from China connected with those that led to the Mediterranean and Rome, provided at least a glimpse of an even more exotic culture. For in the markets of Parthia, the civilizations of the West and the Far East, isolated from each other from the time of their beginnings, met at last.

For two centuries before Alexander's coming, the state of Magadha had been foremost among the kingdoms and tribal confederacies of northeastern India. It not only enjoyed the riches the Greek Megasthenes so glowingly described, it occupied a highly strategic location, astride the Ganges River trade routes and their connection at the river's delta with the Bay of Bengal. From this position, Magadha extended its influence along the eastern coast of India and beyond.

This was the target young Chandragupta Maurya fixed on when he set off on his quest for power. Perhaps inspired by Alexander's campaign in northwestern India, Chandragupta somehow raised an army and in about 324 BC launched it against the Greek garrisons that the Macedonian had left behind in the Punjab and Sindh. His soldiers were probably equipped with a device of awesome power: the massive Indian bow, as tall as a man and so strong that the archer had to use both hands to draw the string, while standing on one foot with the other outstretched to brace the weapon. The arrows were a full nine feet long and capable of piercing the stoutest shield or breastplate.

It was clear from the start that Chandragupta Maurya was a military genius. He soon made himself master of northern India. In his conquest of the Magadhan territories, his strategy was guided, it was said, by a maternal dictum that one should always eat from the edges of one's plate, never beginning at the center. He chipped away at the outlying territory, and before long deposed the last of the Nanda monarchs, who had ruled Magadha for more than half a century. His domain now extended across most of northern India, about 1,300 miles from the western tributaries of the Indus to the eastern reaches of the Ganges.

The Elephant at War

The armies of Chandragupta Maurya included a formidable type of heavy cavalry: thundering herds of elephants ridden by armed Indian warriors. So terrifying were the huge beasts that even well-disciplined Greek phalanxes had quailed before them, and Alexander, impressed with their effect, had incorporated war elephants into his own military forces.

In time, elephant cavalry was adopted by armies throughout the Middle East. But the Indians remained the most adept at capturing wild elephants and training them for battle. Soothing songs and music were used to pacify them, and good behavior was reinforced by rewards not only of food but of flowers, of which the creatures seemed particularly fond.

Before going into battle the elephants were painted with garish colors and given large quantities of rice wine to increase their aggressiveness. In addition to a driver, known as the mahout, Indian war elephants carried one to three soldiers, who were usually equipped with shields and quivers of bamboo spears. But it was the animal itself, as it lunged with its tusks, the bronze bell around its neck clanging, that proved the most fearsome weapon.

Chandragupta's conquests had brought under his sway a multitude of peoples of widely diverse races, languages, religions, and cultures, and he meant to forge them into a single, unified state. In this design, the wealth of Magadha would serve him well. Commerce and industry flourished throughout that kingdom. Magadhan artisans manufactured jewelry, perfumes, fine fabrics, leatherwork, pottery, garments, and the like, while foundries turned out swords, arrowheads, and other weapons of war. Caravans of bullock carts and flotillas of riverboats carried these and other goods throughout the country and to and from the seaports in the east. The state owned all mines, shipyards, armaments factories, and many of the textile-making enterprises. And it levied taxes on virtually all forms of wealth — including livestock, gold, and the proceeds of trade.

Beyond the trading routes and factory towns, Magadha, like the rest of India, was a country of settled farmers gathered in small villages. The Nandas had organized a highly efficient tax-collection bureaucracy to ensure that the state got its share of the value of the crops. Chandragupta outdid them; he not only claimed a tax of one-quarter or more of the value of the harvests, but taxed the land as well. His treasury grew fabulously rich. Apparently the heavy taxation caused little or no unrest, perhaps because the peasants were long used to the attentions of the tax collector.

Under Chandragupta, the Mauryan capital at Pataliputra took its place among the largest and finest cities in the world. Its multistory houses, built of wood and mud brick for easy replacement after the frequent floods, sprawled over twelve square miles along the south bank of the Ganges, near its confluence with the Son River. Enclosed by a great wall of timbers bristling with 570 watchtowers, the city was further protected by a moat 900 feet wide and 45 feet deep.

Chandragupta used his wealth to build an enormous bureaucracy, the most complex and sophisticated that India had ever seen. Whereas cities traditionally had been administered by a council composed of five elders, Chandragupta installed six such boards in his capital — one each to oversee industrial arts, regulate commerce, collect a 10 percent sales tax, see to the comfort of foreigners, record births and deaths, and supervise the maintenance of public places.

The ruler was guided in these moves by his cunning and devoted prime minister, Kautilya, an elder possessed of a subtle and devious mind. Kautilya made an early contribution to a written summary of Indian wisdom that in later centuries, with many additions, was to become the Arthashastra — literally, "The Science of Material Gain." It dealt at length with the accumulation and exercise of power.

What Chandragupta had created, and the Arthashastra later extolled, was a sort of benevolent despotism. Virtually every aspect of an individual's behavior — from practicing a trade to observing a religion, from learning etiquette to settling family differences, from entering a monastery to engaging the help of a witch — was considered a proper area for state control.

The Arthashastra taught that since men are by nature fickle and temperamental, they should be "constantly kept under vigilance in their duties." They should be allowed neither dispute nor unity, for disputes hampered their work and unity threatened the state. Such close control of subordinates required not only minute supervision, but spies — spies in all walks of life, women as well as men, spies everywhere, so many

105

that they came to be regarded as a separate class of society. Many were trained from childhood for the profession, and some were assigned to spy on other spies.

This pervasive involvement of the state with private life was mitigated somewhat by a tolerance for certain types of private enterprise and considerable local autonomy within the guidelines. Many guilds and communities enjoyed a wide freedom to manage their own affairs. Moreover, common subjects could take solace in knowing that the king himself was in no way exempt from duty to the state. One text stipulated what the king was expected to do during every moment of the day and night, specifying the hours for receiving subjects, meeting with the council, attending to domestic duties, praying, and inspecting and managing the armed forces. Once a day and once each night, he was to receive reports from his spies; a separate time was allotted for sending them out.

Chandragupta and his successors devoted much of their wealth to building military power. At the height of the Mauryan empire, its army was counted at 600,000 infantry, 30,000 cavalry, 9,000 war elephants, and 8,000 chariots. The armed forces were run by six boards of five members each, which divided responsibilities for the infantry, navy, cavalry, elephants, chariots, and supply.

The king was not expected to oversee his huge governmental structure alone. "A single wheel can never move," observed the Arthashastra; "hence the king shall employ ministers and hear their opinion." They should be appointed according to merit, "not on the considerations of family, or backstairs influence," and only after rigorous checking by royal spies.

Chandragupta had about seventeen years to consolidate his power in northern India before he faced his first outside challenge. It was a formidable one. In 305 BC, Seleucus Nicator, the Greek general who after Alexander's death had won control of much of western Asia, from Syria to Afghanistan, moved a force into the Punjab and confronted the rising Mauryan empire.

The eventual peace treaty between the two powers did not relate whether they actually fought or whether they settled their differences by threat and negotiation. If they met in battle, it must have been a titanic clash. Seleucus was an able commander with a powerful army; yet Chandragupta not only forced him out of the Punjab, but acquired three of the invader's own rich, adjacent provinces. When a peace agreement was made, Seleucus sent one of his own daughters to Chandragupta, and the Mauryan reciprocated with a troop of 500 magnificent war elephants. Of greater moment, the peace established the western border of the Mauryan empire along the Hindu Kush mountains.

As Chandragupta grew older, he developed a deepening interest in religion. For three centuries, India had been in religious ferment, with several sects challenging the dominant orthodoxy of the Hindu Brahmans. Two of these sects, in particular, had been gaining adherents since the sixth century BC, when Siddhartha Gautama, the founder of Buddhism, had glimpsed the Eightfold Path to enlightenment while sitting under a tree in Magadha, and when his younger contemporary Mahavira had experienced a similar vision that led him to found Jainism.

Both Buddhism and Jainism opposed many of the traditional features of society upheld by the Brahmans, especially the rigid caste system that divided the Indian people into four principal classes, each segregated from the other by custom that had the force of law. At the top were the priestly Brahmans, after whom ranked the Kshatriyas, or warriors and aristocrats. Next came the Vaishyas, the merchants, farmers, and artisans who made up the largest component of Mauryan society, and finally the Sudras, lowly laborers of mixed origins.

The Buddhists and Jains ignored these ancient distinctions. Their monasteries accepted not only men from all walks of life, but also women, and became centers of democratic ideas and education. Those who entered monastic orders of both sects were ascetic, but Jainist monks carried it to an extreme, often going entirely without either clothing or food.

It was Jainism above all that fascinated Chandragupta. According to Jainist tradition, in 301 BC he abdicated in favor of his son Bindusara, entered a Jainist monastery in southern India, and there, in fervent belief, slowly starved himself to death.

During Bindusara's twenty-eight-year reign, he apparently expanded the empire to encompass the vast Deccan plateau that stretches over most of the southern half of the subcontinent, although no record of just how he accomplished this survives. Of the seven male children he fathered, one was described in later legends as being notably homely and roundly disliked by Bindusara. But the boy's mother, who may have been a Greek princess, described herself on the occasion of his birth as being "without sorrow," probably meaning she was pleased to have borne a son. The word she used — Asoka — became the child's name.

Despite his father's distaste — or perhaps because of it — the young Asoka was made viceroy of an outlying province as soon as he came of age. He proved to be a shrewd and tough-minded leader. And when the death of Bindusara triggered a vicious, four-year war of succession, it was Asoka who emerged as the victor, having slain, legend said, all but one of his brothers.

He was to be the most remarkable of all the Mauryan emperors. Ascending the throne in 269 BC, Asoka spent eight years consolidating his power, then invaded Kalinga on India's east coast, the last major independent kingdom on the subcontinent. After a long and bloody war, in which 100,000 soldiers died and 150,000 people were taken captive and deported, Kalinga was brought into the Mauryan empire.

The details of the war, as well as Asoka's philosophy, were recorded for the ages in a series of inscriptions that Asoka ordered carved in stone throughout his empire. These 5,000 words were inscribed on a number of large boulders and thirty pillars erected for the purpose. According to these Rock Edicts, as they are called, Asoka experienced great remorse after the conquest of Kalinga. "The slaughter, death, and carrying away captive of the people," read one of the inscriptions, "is a matter of profound sorrow and regret to His Sacred Majesty." So contrite was Asoka that in the tenth year of his reign, he adopted Buddha's law of nonviolence. Forever after, the emperor rejected the cynical manipulations of the Arthashastra and preached a radical new notion of government, one based on morality and social compassion, in which the king held his power in trust for all living creatures.

Asoka's new attitude may have been based on religion, but it also contained a strong element of shrewd practicality. The Mauryan empire now encompassed all of India, except for three small kingdoms in the south. As the first universal emperor of India, Asoka was master of perhaps 50 million people separated by great distances, by many widely different languages, by religions and customs, and, in some cases, by fierce feelings of independence. What India needed now was a common identity and purpose. To this end, the wise Asoka rejected control by force and spies and instead spoke of all Indians as "my children," for whom he desired "every kind of welfare and happiness both in this world and the next."

He used his wealth in practical applications of his words. He opened the royal vaults to build hospitals and veterinary clinics that served his subjects without charge. He built fine roads to improve communications and trade among the various parts of his empire, and along them he erected rest houses for travelers. In his quest for unity, Asoka established the Prakrit tongue as the official language of his empire — except in the far northwest, where Greek, too, was officially recognized.

He paid little attention to caste, and although the philosophy he espoused was primarily Buddhist in its tenets, he remained on good terms with Jains and Hindu Brahmans. It was Buddhism, however, that benefited most from his success. Aided by his support and disseminated by his expanding trade network, the faith spread beyond India to dominate Asia and become one of the great religions of the world.

Instead of sending military forces to impose his will within the empire, Asoka dispatched civil administrators, called "overseers of the law" or "high commissioners of equity," to the various provinces to supervise local officials. These internal ambassadors were trained to know and respect the customs of various minorities and to pay special attention to their needs. The army, meanwhile, was concentrated on the northwestern frontier to guard against invasion.

Asoka traveled extensively, cultivating his image as father of his people. "Both this world and the other are hard to reach," he admonished his subjects, "except by great love of the law, great self-examination, great obedience, great respect, great energy. This is my rule: government by the law, administration according to the law, gratification of my subjects under the law, and protection through the law."

Asoka maintained diplomatic and trade relations with the remnants of Alexander's empire — Syria, Egypt, Macedonia, and Cyrene. To these states India dispatched caravans laden with spices, precious gems, perfumes, silk, and ivory, importing in exchange linen, glass vessels, precious metals, and medicinal herbs. Meanwhile Asoka's ambassadors, at his direction, informed the world that he had renounced warfare — which beyond his borders was taken more as a sign of weakness than enlightenment. Ambitious men took note for the future.

For the moment, however, India enjoyed its wealth in peace and tranquility. Life was marked by rectitude and order. There apparently was little theft, and many people left their homes and property unguarded. Truth and honor were greatly prized, but they were also backed up by severe laws. Mutilation was the punishment for bearing false witness. An individual who maimed another person was sentenced to lose the same limb plus a hand. And whoever caused an artisan to lose an eye or a hand was put to death. Curiously, there was no remedy at law for bad debts; the creditor apparently had only himself to blame for trusting a rogue.

The conditions of private life seem to have been peaceful. Marriage was usually arranged. Marriageable maidens were exhibited in public by their fathers to be selected by the victors in running, wrestling, or other manly competitions. At other times, a suitor simply offered his prospective in-laws a yoke of oxen for their daughter's hand. Indian women were virtuous, although at least one European writer asserted that even a paragon might grant her favors in exchange for an elephant — perhaps less an indication of the high value of elephants than of the low regard that men traditionally have had for the morals of women of a different culture.

Indians ate sensibly and well, most often rice, topped with a variety of vegetables and fish, or occasionally meat. There apparently were no special mealtimes, people instead eating whenever they were hungry. The rich ate from gold bowls, and other-

Concerned for the welfare of his subjects, the Mauryan ruler Asoka established rest stops for travelers *(left)* along the empire's highways. In addition to wells and lodging, many of the wayside resting places had monumental columns on which were carved verses of Buddhist doctrine, as well as inspirational edicts from Asoka.

wise displayed their wealth with earrings of ivory, shoes of fine white leather, and robes worked in gold thread and ornamented with precious stones. A fashionable man might dye his beard blue, red, purple, or even green. Common folk wore plain cotton garments, sometimes for men a simple loincloth, or dhoti. And Indians of any substance carried parasols to shield themselves from the blazing sun. To keep fit, the wealthy rolled their bodies with small, hand-held ebony rollers, or had servants do it for them. The king sometimes had a roller massage while giving an audience.

In this more or less relaxed and benign atmosphere, technology and art came to flower as never before. Asoka's pillars were prodigious feats; forty to fifty feet high and weighing fifty tons, each monolith was polished to a mirror finish and surmounted by an enormous stone capital exquisitely carved with the figures of lions, elephants, bulls, or religious symbols — probably crafted by Persian stoneworkers, famous for their skill. As monuments to a glorious empire, they would remain for two millennia. In the capital of Pataliputra, the palaces were adorned so lavishly that a Chinese pilgrim named Fa-hien, visiting the city centuries later, believed them to be of supernatural origin: "The royal palace and halls in the midst of the city were all made by spirits which Asoka employed, and which piled up the stones, reared the walls and gates, and executed the elegant carving and inlaid sculpture work in a way which no human hands of this world could accomplish."

Asoka put the talents of innumerable architects and builders at the service of religion. A profusion of monasteries rose throughout the empire, along with thousands of masonry domes known as stupas — which housed relics or marked locations that were sacred to Buddhists and Jains.

The great emperor died in 232 BC after a reign of nearly four decades. Many sons competed bitterly for the right to succeed him, and in the ensuing chaos, the empire began to disintegrate. In the absence of Asoka's remarkable religious and political authority, ancient internal rivalries flared, and outside enemies renewed their long-delayed attacks. Rich as it was, the economy faltered under the combined effects of political uncertainty and the staggering costs of maintaining both the massive bureaucracy and a hastily enlarged military force.

Yet the sons of Asoka clung to the imperial throne for another forty-eight years, until in 184 BC the last of the Mauryan kings was assassinated — in front of his own army, by its Brahman commander. After 140 years, the Mauryan rule of a united India came to an end, and a new era of independent rajas began. Meanwhile, to the west, another empire was on the rise.

The lands that extended westward from the Hindu Kush to the shores of the Black Sea and the Mediterranean were not so beneficent as those of India. Towering mountains ringed a high plateau — saline, rocky, and arid, bitterly cold in winter and searingly hot in summer when the terrible Wind of 120 Days scoured the desert.

The climate was kinder in other parts of the region. Along the Caspian Sea, there was ample rainfall, allowing lush vegetation to flourish. But the real prize lay to the southwest: There, across thousands of square miles, spread the enormously fertile flood plain of the Tigris and Euphrates rivers, where early farmers first produced an agricultural surplus, where civilization was born, and where covetous armies had surged back and forth ever since.

All of this vast domain had been Alexander's, and after his death it was ruled mainly by his General Seleucus and his successors. But the Seleucids were not cast in Alex-

Faithful Indians meditate before Buddha's empty throne in this sculpture from a Mauryan stupa *(left)*. For the first four centuries of Buddhism, the religion's founder was portrayed only symbolically — as a tree, a wheel, or an invisible presence. It was not until the second century AD that artists began to portray Buddha in human form *(inset)*, often clad in the robes of an Indian prince.

During the reign of Asoka, a wooded hill near the village of Sanchi in north central India was chosen as the site for a monumental shrine dedicated to the teachings of Buddha. There a huge domed building called a stupa was erected to house a portion of Buddha's cremated remains; around it sprang up a spiritual enclave that included Buddhist temples, a monastery, and religious schools. Sanchi became a place of pilgrimage for thousands, one of the holiest places in all of the Mauryan empire.

For Buddhists the Great Stupa at Sanchi was much more than a tomb; its massive and yet intricate construction was intended as a symbolic representation of Buddha's thought. The Stupa's polished sandstone railings and gateways bore beautifully carved allegorical scenes illustrating the life and precepts of Buddha, and the building's circular shape was intended as a literal representation of the circle that in Buddhism symbolized universal enlightenment.

A SHRINE FOR BUDDHA

ander's imperial mold, though they called themselves emperors; they focused their primary attention on the rich western provinces of Syria and Babylonia, while the rest of their legacy gradually crumbled away. By the third century BC, the Punjab had been lost to the Mauryans, and Asia Minor was on the verge of falling piecemeal to local kings. Besides Syria and Babylonia, the principal Seleucid provinces were Persis, in the arid southern Iranian plateau, and — across the dusty northern part of the plateau — Media, Bactria, and Parthia.

In midcentury, at the height of Mauryan reign in India, tribes of fierce nomads from the north started drifting southward into Bactria and Parthia, where they quickly established themselves and challenged the rule of the Seleucids. Among them was a particularly strong and able people known as the Parni, probably descendants or kinspeople of the Scythians who in an earlier era had challenged the might of the old Persian empire. The Parni were superb horsemen and archers. Their leader was a shrewd and ruthless chieftain called Arsaces, who would found a dynasty that would endure well into the Christian era. His very name was to become the title by which generations of high kings would be known.

The Parthians, as the Parni came to be called, left little written record of their remarkable time. But others who came into contact with them made certain to chronicle their doings. The Romans, in particular, were forever engaged with the Parthians, and such writers and historians as Justin, Plutarch, Horace, Cicero, and Tacitus described the empire of the Parthians in great if not highly favorable detail. Other contemporary writers — expatriate Greeks, Jews, and traders from the Orient — filled in a more balanced picture.

The Parthian chieftain, Arsaces, died around 248 BC. Over ensuing generations, the Arsacids who succeeded him ceased functioning as mere tribal chiefs and began to conduct themselves as monarchs. Unlike their nomadic forebears, the heirs of Arsaces established fortified cities throughout central Asia and northeastern Iran and paid ardent attention to the process of expanding their territory. Theirs was always more an imperial confederation than it was an empire ruled firmly by a centralized authority, however. They were careful to win the loyalties — or at least the acquiescence — of the minorities they ruled.

The Parthian horsemen drove westward to the Caspian and beyond, into Media, then were halted by a Seleucid army and suffered another setback when their former ally, Bactria, turned on them. But the Parthians held on to their province and their fierce independence, while awaiting the right time and leader for renewed conquest.

The time arrived in the middle of the second century BC, when the Seleucid empire was staggering before the onslaught of Romans from the west. The Arsacid king was Mithradates, a man of extraordinary ability who was crowned in 171 BC. (Parthian monarchs who bore the name Mithradates were not related to a succession of kings of Pontus in Asia Minor with the same name, who reigned during this same era.) In a brutal war, Mithradates subjugated Media, and around 142 BC, he descended on the fertile valleys of the Tigris and the Euphrates, the very heart of the Seleucid empire. The Seleucid king, Demetrius Nicator, hastily gathered an army and confidently marched east to meet the upstart Parthians. To his amazement, he was outmaneuvered, defeated, and captured, to be paraded on a Parthian leash through the cities he once ruled. Subsequently, however, Demetrius was treated with more compassion; Mithradates gave him a comfortable residence and a daughter to be his wife.

Meanwhile, Mithradates invaded a weakened Bactria in the east and went on to

A statuette commemorates a ruler of Hatra, a prosperous city located between the Tigris and Euphrates rivers in the western portion of the Parthian empire. The king, clad in traditional Parthian costume, holds in his hands an image of the moon god Sin.

push his borders even farther south until the Parthian domain stretched from India to the Euphrates and from the Caspian Sea to the Persian Gulf. The fabled, fertile land of Babylonia was now under Parthian rule. Having inherited a kingdom, Mithradates on his death in 138 BC bequeathed to his son an empire that had become a power in the ancient world.

His young successor, Phraates II, was beset by challenges from nearly all directions. Nomads attacked the empire from the north and east, and the Seleucids continued to pose a threat in the west. The capture of Demetrius had left that empire convulsed in a struggle for succession, which eventually was won by a man who took the name Antiochus VII. Immediately, the new ruler laid plans to invade Parthian territory.

Antiochus had two motives for his attack: to regain Seleucid territory, of course, but also to deal with the former Seleucid ruler, Demetrius Nicator. As long as Demetrius was alive, he represented a threat to whoever occupied the Seleucid throne. Indeed, Phraates had continued to treat his prisoner with exceeding solicitude, possibly with a view to using him as a figurehead in a future invasion of Syria. Demetrius responded to this wooing by repeatedly attempting to escape. But his ever-watchful Parthian captors ran him down each time, and on one occasion, Phraates made him a present of a pair of golden dice — a gentle, symbolic admonition to stop gambling with his life.

The onslaught of Antiochus VII in 130 BC soon put Parthian security in jeopardy. At the head of a massive, superbly equipped army, the Seleucid king dealt the Parthians three resounding defeats, reoccupied Babylonia, and drove into Media. With the onset of winter, the Seleucid army remained in Media, occupying several cities and harshly oppressing the population. In the spring, Antiochus demanded that Phraates turn over Demetrius, surrender all territory outside Parthia itself, and pay him tribute as a vassal.

The Parthian response was swift and devastating. Phraates advanced on the scattered Seleucid forces before they had time to reunite, at the same time fomenting revolts among the oppressed local people. The Seleucid garrisons found themselves everywhere harassed, and when Antiochus rashly advanced against a Parthian host with a ragged and ill-prepared army, his troops were routed and he himself was slain. The Seleucids had lost their eastern provinces for good.

For the Parthians, another challenge was soon pressing. About that time, Saca nomads — displaced from the east by the movements of other peoples — began to migrate into Bactria in large numbers, eventually overrunning that province as well as the Punjab and part of Parthia itself. When Phraates met these invaders in battle in 128 BC, he employed as part of his force the Seleucid Greeks captured in the defeat of Antiochus. The fighting started to go badly for Phraates, and the Greeks immediately turned on him, helping the nomads to slaughter the Parthian army and Phraates as well. It was a lesson the Parthians would long remember.

In time, Phraates' cousin Mithradates II had some success in dealing with the Sacae. While he was unable to halt the invading hordes, he did manage to deflect them south and east, into the Punjab, which they

ROME

BOKHARA

SARDIS

MERV

ANTIOCH

PALMYRA   HAMADAN

TYRE   CHARAX

Campaigning against the fierce Parthians in 53 BC, Roman soldiers noticed that the enemy carried colorful banners of an iridescent material. The Romans learned that the beautiful cloth was silk and that it came from a great kingdom east of Parthia. As the Roman Empire grew in power and wealth, so did the demand for this most luxurious fabric, and a lucrative trade arose between the merchants of the Mediterranean and the far-off empire of China.

Some silk was shipped by sea, but most of it traveled overland via the Silk Road, a tortuous track that wound, fraught with hardship and danger, for 7,000 miles through a half-dozen kingdoms. The camel caravans that carried the silk braved the blizzards of the Himalayas and the sandstorms of the Taklamakan Desert. The greatest threat came from the savage brigands who infested the hills of central Asia. To protect the caravans and keep the route open, detachments of Parthian soldiers patrolled the road through their kingdom. Most of the goods did get through, and with them an awareness and knowledge of peoples a continent away.

TRADING ON THE SILK ROAD

SAMARKAND KASHGAR

TUN-HUANG

MIRAN

LOYANG

CHANG'AN

BARBARIKON

GUANGZHOU

HANOI

gradually wrested from the Indo-Greek dynasts who had succeeded the Mauryans there. The Sacae flourished in that well-watered land and eventually became allies of the Parthians. Meanwhile, Mithradates II restored the empire practically to its former boundaries and expanded north and west, into Armenia.

Although the Parthians did not enjoy a fraction of the natural resources of India, they made much of what they did have. Lacking India's frequent rains, they developed advanced irrigation systems, first using animal power to lift water from the few rivers, then learning to distribute it through sprawling canal networks. To reduce evaporation in the dry heat, they channeled some water through tunnels, in the manner of the ancient Persians. Thanks to these engineering feats, Parthians were able to raise lush crops, fruit and vegetables, as well as rice and other cereal grains, in the relatively arid plains of the Tigris and Euphrates valleys.

In the absence of plentiful ore deposits such as those in India, the Parthians developed little basic manufacturing. They concentrated instead on agriculture and commerce. Herders provided handsome surpluses of sheep, cattle, pigs, and camels, which contributed to Parthia's wealth. But it was as middlemen that the Parthians found the way to true riches.

Under Mithradates II, the Parthian empire for the first time controlled the great trading route that would come to be known as the Silk Road, running between the Roman Empire to the west and China and India to the east. Although the route was doubtless used before the advent of the Parthians, under their unified control and administration it flourished as never before. The volume of trade was soon enormous, and the Parthians took a cut of everything that passed through their territory. A schedule of tariffs listed the tax per camel-load of such items as dried fruits, olive oil, salt, perfumes, bronze statues, precious metals and gems, rugs, and spices — and of course the Chinese silks for which the road was later named.

The society that basked in the glow of this wealth was diverse, vigorous, and well-ordered. Side by side with the Parthians lived the Aramaeans of western Parthia, Babylonians and Jews in Babylonia, and Arabs who wandered the deserts under the watchful eyes of Parthian authorities. Greeks lived in the towns and cities, particularly those founded by Alexander and the Seleucids. In many cases, these peoples had considerable autonomy. The Jews, for example, collected their own community taxes, appointed their own judges, and carried out their own criminal punishments, which included the death penalty.

The Parthians, naturally, were first among equals. The king symbolized their ascendancy; he wore a bejeweled tiara, sat on a golden throne, and slept on a golden couch. He was normally inaccessible; anyone so fortunate as to be granted an audience was required to offer a gift in homage. Possibly because of their nomadic heritage, the Parthian rulers were a restless lot, occasionally moving their capitals. At different times Parthian kings ruled from Nisa on the edge of the Central Asian steppes, Hecatompylos near the Caspian Sea, Ecbatana, the ancient capital of Media, and the city of Ctesiphon, on the Tigris.

The king's subjects, according to Justin and Plutarch, were divided into a minority of freemen — nobles, other aristocrats, and royal officials — and a vast majority of dependents, or serfs, who performed all of the manual labor. Women generally were kept shut away; no woman was allowed to dine with her husband or even to be seen in public. According to Justin, the Parthian male was arrogant, treacherous, and violent, a rather silent sort, quicker to act than to converse. He enjoyed

THE COMPOSITE GODS

As Alexander the Great's many conquests opened avenues of trade eastward, Hellenistic culture spread all the way from the shores of the Mediterranean Sea to the Indian subcontinent. The interaction of the diverse peoples along the trading routes resulted in a fusion of cultures that came to be reflected not only in art and language, but in religion as well. The principal beliefs of Greece and Rome mingled with the religions and cults of various Middle Eastern societies. Foreign gods and goddesses were adopted, given new names, and at times modified in ways that might better suit a particular culture.

In time, as distinctions among the gods were blurred, composite deities came into being. The Greek god Zeus, for example, merged with the Persian Ohrmazd to become Zeus-Oramsdes. Throughout the civilized world, artists gave shape to these borrowed and hybridized gods, some of which appear on these pages.

This bronze is a Parthian version of the Greek hero Herakles, sculpted in the city of Seleucia. In Parthia, Herakles was elevated to divine status and was sometimes depicted as Verethraghna, god of victory.

The principal gods of Greece and Egypt merged to become Zeus-Amon, a deity popular in Egypt during the Roman occupation, when this marble image was sculpted.

A sculpture from Satala in Asia Minor represents the fusion of the Greek goddess Aphrodite with the Persian Anahita, goddess of fertility. Elsewhere Anahita was worshiped as Hera, who was the sister and consort of Zeus.

The Egyptian goddess Isis is shown playing a tambourine and castanets in this stone figure from Byblos in Phoenicia. The cult of Isis spread throughout the Mediterranean during Alexander's time; its followers were later persecuted by imperial Rome.

The proud figure of Athena-
Allat stands accoutered for
war in an ancient Syrian ba-
salt sculpture. Parthians
combined their war god-
dess, Allat, with the Greek
Athena, who traditionally
wore the helmet, cuirass,
and shield embossed with
Medusa's head, as shown.

A carving found in Eng-
land depicts the birth of the
Indo-Parthian god
Mithras, shown emerging
from an egg within a
frame bearing the signs of
the zodiac. The figure
was probably carried to
England by Roman
soldiers who had been ex-
posed to the Mithras
cult while in Parthia.

drink, particularly palm wine, but he was said to eat sparingly: meat from the hunt, some fish, and a few vegetables and grains.

The ordinary homes in Parthian cities were of mud brick, built around a courtyard and lighted at night by many small oil lamps. During the early years of the empire, household vessels were modeled after Greek or Seleucid wares, but gradually Hellenic refinement faded and the shapes became coarser, with blue, green, yellow, or brown glaze and simple decorative grooves and patterns. The rich families of Parthia, of course, lived in much grander style, eating from gold and silver tableware and listening to the music of lyre, pipe, and drum. Palace walls were hung with figured tapestries, and on the floors there lay fine rugs.

In dress, the Parthian upper classes were not averse to a certain flamboyance. Tunics and trousers were trimmed with jewels. Men wore huge decorated belts and sometimes an elaborate coat over the entire ensemble — with leather or cloth leggings for riding, which they were constantly engaged in.

"On horses they go to war, to banquets, to public and private tasks," wrote Justin, "and on them they travel, stay still, do business, and chat." Only slaves went on foot. The chief Parthian love was the hunt, and in later years, a form of polo. As might be expected, no Parthian ruler could be truly acceptable who did not love horses.

For an imperial people, the Parthians were curiously inward looking and relatively uninterested in cultures other than their own. The Greeks of the empire remained in their towns, struggling to preserve what was theirs, and their Hellenistic culture did not greatly affect the mass of the Parthians, although the Greek tongue called Koine was accepted as one of the official languages of the empire.

The Parthians tolerated a wide variety of religions but did not attempt to incorporate religious ideals into government, as Asoka had done in India. The priestly class, called the Magi, maintained the orthodox faith, Zoroastrianism, by this time five centuries old and much diminished from its influential role under the Persians. There was widespread worship of Ahuramazda, identified by Zoroaster as the supreme god, but the important Zoroastrian doctrine of a struggle between good and evil that would be decided at the last judgment was greatly diluted. Parthians apparently were just as likely to worship Mithra, an old pre-Zoroastrian Iranian god identified with the sun, justice, and war. Other cults adapted various Greek deities, similar Oriental gods, or a synthesis of several. Such things were left up to the individual to pursue; the government had more important tasks.

Primary among them was the improvement of the empire's military force. Mithradates II never forgot the treachery of the mercenaries and captured Greeks, and largely eliminated them from the armed forces. Henceforward, the ranks of the army were filled by the peasants and serfs of the great landowners, who were summoned to battle in time of need. Consequently, the army was somewhat provincial and not particularly well trained, but it was Parthian.

Infantry was used for garrison duty and for missions in rough country. But the cavalry was the principal military arm of this horse-oriented people. The heavy cavalry carried enormous lances and was protected by iron chain mail; one type protected just the rider, whereas another draped both mount and man. Formations of these armored horsemen were fearsome against enemy infantry. Yet it was the light cavalry, the horse archers, that made the Parthians legendary in battle. They developed powerful, long-range bows with which they could inflict terrible carnage while safely out of reach of an enemy's arrows. With their skilled horsemanship, they perfected a maneuver much used by Asian nomads — a feigned retreat during which they would launch a deadly backward volley of arrows. The tactic entered several languages as the so-called Parthian shot — later corrupted in English to parting shot.

The Romans came to know this Parthian cavalry and its tactics better than they might have wished. In 96 BC, Mithradates II extended his western boundary to the Euphrates. The next year, the Roman general Sulla arrived at the river, which now became the boundary between the Roman and Parthian empires; the Seleucid empire had been all but crushed out of existence between the two. Mithradates dispatched an ambassador to the Romans to express friendship and a willingness to form an alliance, and Sulla arrogantly took this overture as submission; he had no idea of the military and economic power he was facing. Sulla agreed to the particulars of an alliance, but with such contempt that the humiliated Mithradates II executed his own ambassador for failing to uphold the honor of Parthia.

It was a fragile arrangement to make with such a menacing power, but for a time Rome was far from the worst of the problems that confronted the Parthians. The Arsacid kings had never exercised tight central control over their empire, and around 90 BC, some of their vassals began to challenge Parthian rule. First, Babylonia successfully revolted. Then, after Mithradates II died in 87 BC, Armenia to the north and two provinces in the southeast also broke away. By 66 BC, the area ruled by the Parthians had shrunk substantially and was surrounded by independent kingdoms and states only nominally under Arsacid control. Such an agglomeration was ill prepared to resist the eastward drive of Rome.

In 55 BC, Crassus, a member of the Roman ruling triumvirate, became the governor of Syria. Although he was more than sixty years old at the time, Crassus was consumed with ambition and was determined to eclipse the fame of Caesar, of Pompey, even of Alexander. His route to glory, over the strenuous objections of his fellow Romans, was to be an invasion of Parthia. Crassus moved slowly, edging into northern Mesopotamia in 54 BC while pondering how to attack the distant Parthian city of Seleucia on the Tigris. The Arsacid king, Orodes, sent an ambassador to inquire whether Crassus was approaching on behalf of Rome, in which case he would be opposed without quarter, or on some private mission, in which case he would be pitied for his senility. Crassus haughtily replied that he would give his answer in Seleucia. Orodes' ambassador, perhaps mindful of the fate of an earlier emissary who had accepted insult from Rome, extended his hand and proclaimed, "Hair, Crassus, will grow on my palm before you see Seleucia."

In the spring of 53 BC, Crassus crossed the Euphrates with more than 40,000 soldiers and entered northern Mesopotamia. The move caught Orodes with his infantry far to the north, in Armenia, which he had thought was Crassus's true objective. But instead of turning south to take Seleucia, Crassus foolishly decided to pursue a force of 10,000 cavalrymen under a young Parthian nobleman named Suren, which was falling back to the east. As Sulla had been before him, Crassus was ignorant of the abilities of the troops he was confronting.

Crassus chased the mounted Parthians with his foot soldiers, denying his increasingly hungry and weary men the rest they needed. Suddenly, on a hot afternoon, the Parthian horsemen turned and swept down on the Romans. Crassus desperately tried to form his troops into an enormous square — the standard Roman defensive formation — but the Parthian heavy-cavalry lancers, in their mailed armor, drove into the

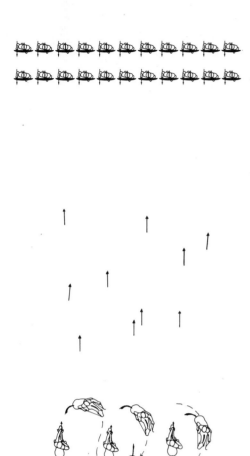

The bulk of the Parthian army was composed of skilled horsemen who ranked among the finest cavalry in the ancient world. The heavy cavalry, or *Clibinarii* — one of whom is shown in the frieze at left — were the army's shock troops. The typical Clibinarius wore an iron helmet, was heavily armored in a suit of chain mail, and wielded a lance from the back of a huge, armor-clad horse. In contrast, Parthian light cavalry — the *Cataphracti* — were clad in loose cloth tunics and trousers, rode small, agile mounts, and were armed with long-range bows and quivers of arrows *(inset, left)*. In battle the horse archers made deadly use of hit-and-run tactics *(diagram, above)*, loosing their arrows as they galloped to within fifty yards of an enemy line *(top)*, then wheeling to the right while continuing to fire "Parthian shots" as they withdrew. Once the enemy ranks showed confusion, the Parthian heavy cavalry, who were stationed behind the horse archers, moved in for the kill. Such tactical skill enabled Parthian armies to vanquish even the vaunted legions of Rome.

lightly armed Romans and made it impossible for them to complete the square.

Then the heavy cavalry fell back, making way for the mounted archers, who surrounded the Roman legions and unleashed a terrible hail of arrows. With their powerful bows, the Parthian horsemen were able to pierce Roman armor while riding safely beyond range of the enemy. When the frustrated Roman foot soldiers charged, trying to grapple with their elusive opponents, the Parthian cavalry simply retired, volleying Parthian shots as they rode off.

The Roman officers remained confident, although their men were falling like wheat before the reaper. The Parthians, the Roman leaders assured themselves, would soon run out of arrows, and then the invincible legions would close with the enemy, hurl their javelins, and engage with their short swords, destroying these barbarians as they had destroyed so many others. The Romans began to lose heart only when they observed the arrival of a Parthian supply; according to later reports, there were 1,000 camels laden with a fresh supply of arrows.

Meanwhile the Romans still had not been able to complete their defensive square, and now one of their exposed flanks was being turned. Crassus ordered his son Publius to drive off the enemy long enough for the beleaguered legions to close ranks.

Publius disappeared into the dust, at the head of nearly 4,000 running, cheering men. At last, Crassus was able to complete his square — only to receive an urgent message from Publius calling for help. Once again, the Parthians had melted away before the onslaught, and then flowed in at the flanks and rear until the charging Romans were halted and surrounded, immobile under a lethal storm of arrows. While organizing a rescue attempt, Crassus saw a triumphant Parthian ride into sight brandishing a lance; impaled on its tip was the severed head of his son Publius.

The slaughter continued until nightfall. Crassus was incapacitated by grief, humiliation, and despair. His officers ordered a retreat to the nearby walled town of Carrhae, which was accomplished in the dark to the anguished screams of whatever was left of the 4,000 wounded men dying at the hands of the vengeful Parthians. In the town, the Romans soon found themselves surrounded again, without food or hope of relief.

Their only chance to escape was again by night. A few got away, including an officer named Cassius, later to play a prominent role in the assassination of Julius Caesar. But Crassus and the main part of the army were caught and surrounded yet again. Suren demanded that Crassus meet him to negotiate a treaty.

Somehow, whether through treachery or a misunderstanding, a fracas broke out during the parley. Instead of taking Crassus's surrender, Suren took his head, and sent it to Orodes. Only a quarter of the Roman army escaped. Twenty thousand had been killed, and ten thousand were taken prisoner; the captives ultimately were settled in the farthest reaches of the Parthian empire. Crassus had achieved his immortality — as architect of one of the greatest military disasters in the history of Rome. The Parthians now became known as Rome's equal, and the Euphrates was established for more than a century as the immutable boundary between the empires.

Suren enjoyed his triumph only briefly; Orodes thought him entirely too capable an underling and had him murdered. There followed a period of armed truce with the Romans and intrigue among the Parthians. Eventually, the mistrustful Orodes lost his mind and abdicated in favor of a savage son, who killed his father and some thirty brothers to secure the throne.

The reign of this new emperor, Phraates IV, was so harsh that a Parthian noble convinced the Roman commander Mark Antony of an easy conquest in Parthia. In the spring of 36 BC, Mark Antony led an army of 100,000 men into Media, driving toward the Parthian heartland. But as Crassus had before him, he committed a major error; he divided his forces, leaving part of his infantry behind to escort the slow-moving baggage train and siege engines. These Phraates IV found and attacked with total success, killing 10,000 Roman troops and destroying Mark Antony's supplies and equipment.

Meanwhile Mark Antony found himself harassed by the redoubtable Parthian cavalry, unable to forage for supplies, unable to negotiate a truce. Facing in addition the rigors of approaching winter, he had to retreat. It was a death march, the men dropping from hunger and disease as well as from Parthian arrows. In all, Mark Antony lost more than 35,000 men — one-third of his army — in Parthia. Then, when the diminished legions had stumbled across a river that marked the empire's border, the Parthian horsemen who had pursued them suddenly unstrung their bows, praised the Romans for their fortitude, and went home. Mark Antony headed for Egypt and the soothing attentions of Queen Cleopatra.

Never again would the Romans mount a serious incursion east of the Tigris, although skirmishes would persist as long as the two empires existed. They did, however, once play a distant role in Parthia's convoluted and violent brand of politics.

During an interlude of more-or-less friendly relations, the Roman emperor Augustus sent a slave girl named Musa to the harem of his Parthian counterpart. The wily concubine gave birth to a prince, persuaded her king to send his older sons to Rome for their safety, then poisoned the king and engineered the succession of her son, whom she subsequently married. Thus, in a few years, Musa rose from chattel to Queen.

Her reign was brief. Within two years, by around AD 4, she and her husband/son had been driven from the throne. But she was not soon to be forgotten. The princes sent at her instigation to Rome became the source of an entirely new succession of contenders for the throne of Parthia. Some of them ruled for a time, only to fall out of favor because of their Western ways; one of them even proved, to the disgust of his subjects, to be uninterested in horses.

The incessant struggle for the throne coupled with the growing power of local rulers undermined Arsacid authority, and the Parthian domain gradually decayed into eighteen loosely affiliated kingdoms. The Parthians managed to maintain a shell of empire for about two centuries, winning a province from the Romans here and losing another to them there, but never recovered their former vitality.

There was, however, to be a final Parthian shot. When Roman legions managed to sack Seleucia in AD 165, one of their number contracted a strange and hideous disease that had been spreading along the Silk Road and had contributed to the weakness of the Parthians. It was probably what later came to be called smallpox. The epidemic swept through the Romans, driving them from Parthia again, and this time they took the enemy home with them. In the years to come the Great Pestilence, as it was called, killed as much as one-quarter of the residents of some Roman cities and played a major role in bringing the Roman Empire to its end.

Meanwhile Parthia followed Mauryan India into obscurity, receding from the dusty and violent stage it had so long and so thoroughly dominated.

THE AGE OF OPULENCE

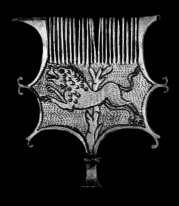

In 150 BC, silver was so rare in Rome that members of a visiting delegation from Carthage, entertained in turn by the capital's leading families, found themselves dining off the same silver dinnerware every night. Roman patricians would not have to endure such embarrassments for long. Four years later, Carthage was leveled by Roman legions, and Greece, the Mediterranean world's acknowledged center of artistic innovation and elegant living, came under Roman rule with the capture of Corinth.

Suddenly, Rome was deluged with untold treasures: priceless paintings and sculpture, finely carved furniture, exotic perfumes, rare spices, and exquisite jewelry in silver and gold. Insatiable appetites for luxuries were whetted by this war booty, and the economic boom that followed the military triumphs made many Romans rich enough overnight to indulge their newfound tastes. "The city," lamented the disapproving writer Pliny, "learned not just to admire foreign opulence but to love it."

While some crusty patricians scoffed at the new ostentation, the newly rich acquired valuables, like those shown on the following pages, with a vengeance, hoping to gain through envy or admiration the social standing their plebeian birth had denied them. They scoured the Mediterranean for the unique and the rare "like hunting dogs," wrote the critic Cicero, "sniffing down every trail, following every trifling clue."

When the supply of precious art and objects dwindled, these patrons imported artisans, setting them up in studios to make copies of coveted originals, as well as splendid and costly household items and personal ornaments like the comb above.

Inevitably, obsession led to excess. A small amber figurine, complained Pliny, cost more than several slaves. A pair of silver cups sold for 100,000 sesterces — a year's pay for a company of legionaries. One collector ordered exquisite relief scenes chiseled off ancient gold cups and incorporated into tasteless modern copies.

The hunger for luxuries was equally strong in the far-flung corners of the Roman world. A Roman governor, anxious to impress his German subjects, embarked on a military campaign with 12,000 pieces of silver tableware. And a satrap in Asia Minor offered 600,000 denarii — a sum equal to the value of 10,000 oxen — for a Greek painting of Dionysus.

Despite the intemperance of some enthusiasts, knowledgeable Romans gradually developed elegant taste. Within a single generation, a spirit of opulence pervaded Roman life, from the private dressing rooms of princesses and matrons to public military and religious spectacles. Temples glittered with gold and silver offerings of wealthy donors, and parading legions jingled with silver swords and gilded armor.

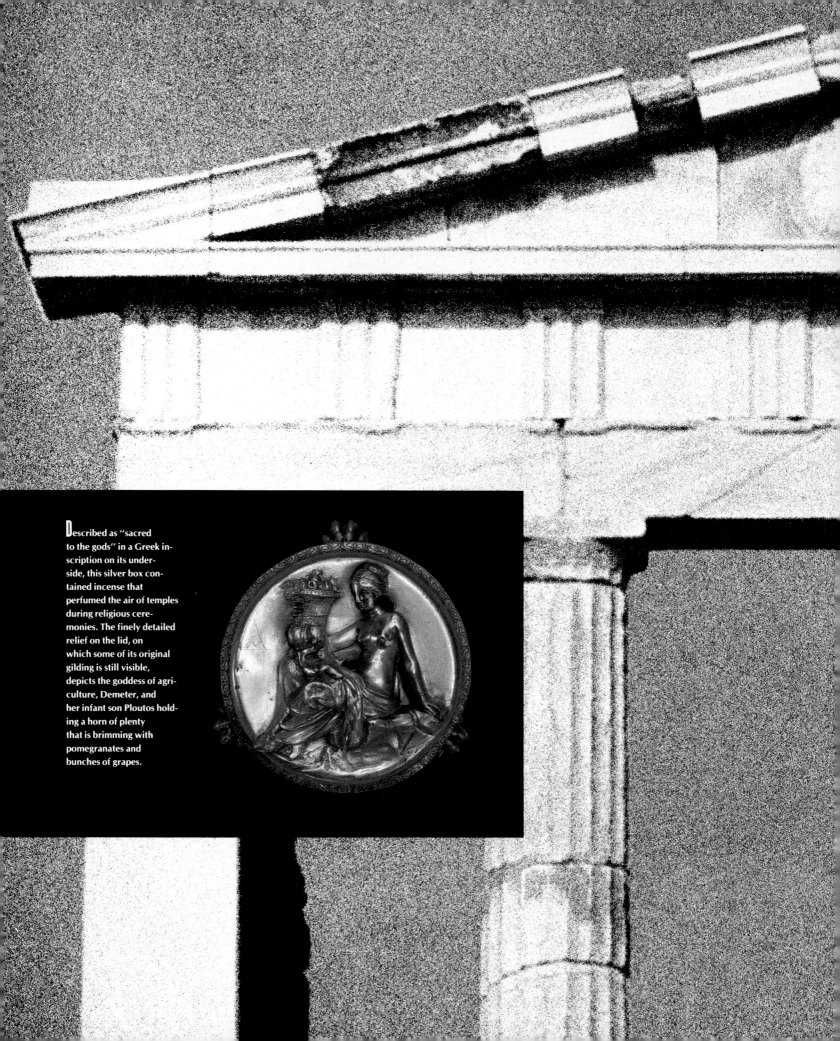

Described as "sacred to the gods" in a Greek inscription on its underside, this silver box contained incense that perfumed the air of temples during religious ceremonies. The finely detailed relief on the lid, on which some of its original gilding is still visible, depicts the goddess of agriculture, Demeter, and her infant son Ploutos holding a horn of plenty that is brimming with pomegranates and bunches of grapes.

A golden offering to the goddess Demeter, a wheat stalk, demonstrates both the sumptuous elegance of religious art and the passion for realistic detail common to Mediterranean goldsmiths. Gold spheres wired to central stems represent the wheat kernels, from which thread-thin gold wires emerge to mimic the grain's fibers.

Hollowed out of crystalline rock called sardonyx, a first century BC drinking cup is appropriately carved with masks of the wine god, Bacchus, and a sideboard set for a feast. The writer Pliny claimed that one Roman was so obsessed with a similar cup that he gnawed away its rim from excessive use.

A solid silver drinking horn, shaped by fourth century BC artisans into a graceful deer's head, is further enriched with gilding on the antlers, ears, rim, and relief scenes of battling warriors. Popular in the Greek world, such creative silverwork later became the rage of Roman collectors, who paid the asking price for any original — extra if it bore signs of prolonged use.

A marriage of form and function, this blown-glass bird graced a first century AD dressing table as a perfume bottle. The container was sealed with molten glass after it was filled. The perfume was released by breaking the tip of the bird's tail.

A silver comb-and-hairpin from first century BC Rome is decorated with engravings of a winged Cupid hunting a lion. These fashionable accessories decorated and held together the elaborate coiffures of some Roman matrons, who favored intricate, high-rising styles evocatively described by the writer Juvenal as "tiers and stories piled one upon another."

Reflecting the prosperity of the wealthy Roman
community where it
was used, a silver mirror
from Pompeii displays,
in a relief carving on its
back, the type of youth-
ful feminine profile its own-
er might have hoped to
see in the polished silver
surface on its front.

An impish satyr, the goat-man that attended the Roman god Bacchus, grins in finely carved relief on a first century BC sardonyx cameo signed by the engraver Hyllos. Along with his father, Dioskourides, a widely acclaimed and honored craftsman who carved the imperial seal of Augustus, Hyllos eschewed the common practice of leaving artwork unsigned.

Alternate settings of emeralds and pearls add color and contrast to the gold mesh pattern of a first century AD necklace. Precious stones and organic materials such as pearls were first incorporated into jewelry designs by innovative Greek artisans, who imported rich green emeralds from Egypt and luminous white pearls from India.

A garnet-studded Herakles knot, ancient symbol of love's binding strength, ties the gold filigree headband of a fourth century BC diadem from a Greek colony on the Black Sea. When fastened with pins over a high-piled hairstyle, the diadem embellished a royal lady's head with an array of gold, garnet, agate, and carnelian pendants.

A gilded bronze scabbard, embossed with symbols of military triumph, was presented to a legionary after Tiberius, stepson of the emperor Augustus, defeated a marauding Celtic tribe in 15 BC. Such richly decorated weapons rewarded past heroism and inspired the possessor to greater deeds.

Glittering *goryti* like this one, bow and arrow cases favored by Scythian archers, were valued war trophies. This gorytus was buried in the tomb of a fourth century BC Greek king, who likely captured it in battle. Made of gilded silver, it is embossed with intricate designs and bloody battle scenes in which civilians flee before sword-wielding invaders.

THE FLOWERING OF CHINA

Far beyond the eastern rim of the Roman world, beyond the fields of Parthia and the Ganges Plain and the central Asian steppes, another people, the Chinese, were building an empire of their own. And for a time in this imperial age — after the collapse of Alexander's dominion and before the apogee of Rome's — theirs was the greatest empire on earth, although few in the Western world were even aware of it. The Chinese were already in firm control of a vast and populous part of East Asia when the Romans first set out to conquer the eastern end of the Mediterranean, a much smaller region. Even as Rome neared the zenith of its power, its empire did not significantly surpass China's in extent or wealth. And the flourishing civilization that had originated in north China's valleys and plains spread throughout eastern Asia much more pervasively, more thoroughly reshaping the indigenous societies in its image, than did Rome's Greco-Roman culture in the West.

It was during this era of expansion that China reached and defined the borders it would maintain more or less continuously ever after. Self-sufficient and self-contained, the imperial nation made sporadic forays beyond the walls it erected along those borders but channeled most of its energy inward, cultivating a stability and uniformity of culture, economy, and social structure that were without parallel among the ancient empires. It was then, too, that China established the multilayered bureaucracy that would remain, through the passing ages, a constant in Chinese life. (In AD 2 those meticulous bureaucrats counted 57,671,400 inhabitants of China, at a time when the Roman Empire's population was probably seven million.)

This was also a time of remarkable achievement in other areas of Chinese life. China's architects and engineers built not only the Great Wall but countless roads, canals, irrigation systems, and immense, fantastically elaborate palaces and tombs. The country's scientists and manufacturers outdid their Western contemporaries in invention and technological progress, and other creative Chinese left a splendid heritage of works in literature and the visual arts. Later generations would come to look back on the major part of this era — the four centuries when their land was ruled by the Han dynasty — as a time of power and glory, orderly growth, and sublime accomplishment. But before then, China experienced almost 200 years of turmoil that followed the collapse of the old Zhou dynasty. During this so-called Warring States Period, feuding kingdoms fought for dominance until one leader and his people won control and forcibly fused China into a single empire.

The people were the Qin, rough and ready products of a rugged land. Their home territory in northwest China was a mountain-ringed fortress known as "the land within the passes," drained by the Wei River and abutting the northern territory — later to be known as Mongolia — which was controlled by hard-riding barbarian tribes who were China's most persistent enemies. The Qin themselves were disparaged as little better

139

than savages by more sophisticated people in other feudal domains. "Qin has the heart of a tiger or a wolf," said one noble from a rival state. "It is avaricious, perverse, and without sincerity. It knows nothing about etiquette, proper relationships, and virtuous conduct."

The Qin did know warfare, however. Superb with sword and crossbow, they repelled their foes' attempts to penetrate their highland province, even when five other states joined together against them in 318 BC. The Qin scorned the gentlemanly style of war that had prevailed earlier in China. Their troops were paid bounties for the heads of enemy soldiers, and after one victory over an army from the state of Zhao in 234 BC, the triumphant Qin reportedly decapitated 100,000 men. When the protracted period of intermittent warfare finally reached its critical final years, the Qin, in the apt metaphor of one chronicler, "ate up its neighbors as a silkworm devours a leaf." One by one the warring kingdoms succumbed to their might — the Hann and the Wei to the east, the Chu in the south, the Yan in the northeast, and finally, in 221 BC, the Qi in eastern China. All China now lay at the feet of the Qin monarch.

The stories about the man who now proclaimed himself the first emperor of a united China and took the name Shi huangdi — literally First August Sovereign, or First Emperor — portrayed him as an outsize villain, a cruel, impetuous, and superstitious tyrant who ruled by terror and whim. This may be in part because the history of his regime was written by his enemies, the Han, who succeeded him in power. In their descriptions he was "pigeon breasted, stingy, cringing, graceless," and given to monstrous and inexplicable acts. When a meteor fell to earth and an anonymous citizen wrote

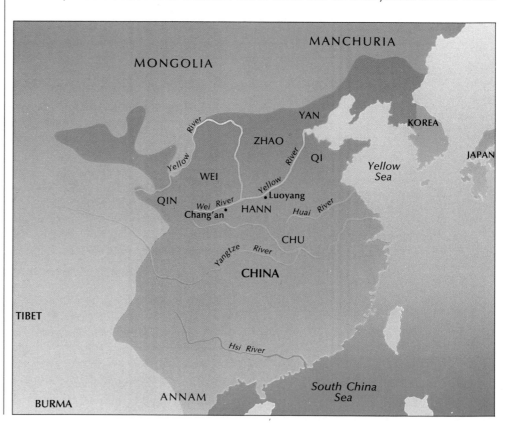

From a collection of warring states, China was unified in 221 BC under its first emperor, Shi huangdi of the Qin dynasty. In his regime, disparate sections of the Great Wall were connected and the wall was extended across the northern frontier as protection against the marauding Xiongnu tribes of Mongolia. The Qin also advanced China's borders to the south into what later became Vietnam and to the northeast into Korea. The Han dynasty, which succeeded the Qin, tightened China's grip on those territories and reached into the west to claim a finger of Tibet.

anti-imperial messages on it, said Han historians, the emperor ordered the execution of everyone living nearby. They alleged that in his later years he was so security-conscious that he changed sleeping quarters nightly, and decreed death for anyone who disclosed his nocturnal whereabouts.

The emperor and his chief minister, named Li Si, were disciples of a doctrine called legalism, which held that people could best be controlled through strict laws and severe punishments. Those guilty of the most serious offenses were beheaded, chopped in half at the waist, or boiled in an enormous caldron. Legalist principles contrasted with the more humane teachings of Confucius, the sage whose ideas were later adopted by the Han, although he died 277 years before that dynasty was founded.

Once established in power, the First Emperor and Li Si set about dismantling the feudal structure of local kings and noble families that had long held sway in the Chinese countryside, replacing it with a strong central government. This was in effect a revolution from the top, and it permanently transformed the way the country was ruled. It was the independent feudal nobles who had diluted the power of the Zhou dynasty a few centuries earlier, causing China's decline into a welter of contentious states. One of the new emperor's first acts was to move all the noble families to his capital at Xianyang, where he could keep an eye on them. Han historians, probably stretching the truth, said that 120,000 families were thus transplanted. The weapons of the emperor's former foes were melted down and cast into bells and statues.

The empire of the First August Sovereign was originally composed of thirty-six regional provinces; more were added when new territory was conquered later. Each province was divided into numerous counties or prefectures, which in turn were made up of districts and hamlets, the smallest administrative units. The provinces were governed not by hereditary lords, as the Zhou kingdoms had been, but by officials appointed by the emperor. The emperor's top deputies were his chancellor or prime minister, the military commander in chief, and a "grandee secretary," who oversaw the performance of government officials. Below these was a cabinet of nine ministers with jurisdiction in areas such as justice, ceremonial rites, and the treasury.

The emperor imposed uniformity on his realm. One decree ordered the standardization of characters used in Chinese writing. Another set empire-wide standards for weights and measures. The government proclaimed a uniform legal code throughout the empire and standardized the gauge of wheeled vehicles, which meant that on Chinese roads everyone rolled along in the same ruts, packing them into hard, smooth tracks. Shi huangdi also permitted peasants to own land, a practice he had followed in the Qin kingdom but a departure from the policy of the earlier Shang and Zhou dynasties, where all land was state owned.

The palace complex in Shi huangdi's capital was said to be so lavish that 700,000 convict laborers worked on the construction of the main royal residence, a majestic building that could hold 10,000 people. But despite the pleasures of the palace, the emperor liked nothing better than touring his realm, sometimes incognito, on trips that could last a year or more. He was fond of having tributes to himself inscribed on stone at sites that he visited; one inscription declared that he had "made the world a single family." The emperor's wanderings may also have been prompted by his mystical belief in the "islands of immortals," said to be the home of an elixir that conferred eternal life. According to one account, he dispatched a sea captain in search of the islands. On returning, the captain reported that he had found the islands but was told to come back with "young men and maidens" to exchange for the magic potion. An expedition of 3,000 young Chinese was then sent forth, never to be heard from again. Later, legends arose that said the young people had colonized Japan.

The First Emperor must have been a leader of colossal aspirations. Everything about him, his fears and hatreds as well as his plans and visions, was exaggerated, magnified beyond human scale. Only such a ruler would have undertaken the construction of the Great Wall. Sections of the wall had been built earlier, but it was at Shi huangdi's command that a general named Meng Tian, supervising a work force probably numbering more than a million, extended the wall all the way across China's northern frontier to hold marauding barbarians at bay. Astonishingly, the 2,600-mile-long wall, which ran from the Yellow Sea in the east to the semidesert Turkestan region in the west, apparently was completed in just seven years.

The Qin left no account as to exactly how they did it, no record of the building techniques, nor any mention of the cost in lives, which must have been enormous for a project of that magnitude. Somehow they set large stone blocks into parallel furrows and faced them with brick, then rammed earth or clay into the space between the blocks. They erected forty-foot-high towers every few hundred yards, the distance said to be calculated at two arrow shots, thus ensuring that any enemy attacking the wall would be within archer range of a tower. No records survived to explain how General Meng fed his immense army of laborers or transported the stones. Ambitious building projects were apparently a Qin specialty. During Shi huangdi's reign, another huge force of workers dug a twenty-mile-long barge canal linking two Yangtze Valley rivers that flowed in opposite directions. The Magic Transport Canal, as it was called, made possible barge navigation over 1,250 continuous miles of inland waterway, and would still be in regular use in the late twentieth century AD.

The armies of Qin, having conquered all the lands then considered Chinese, pushed beyond them to rout neighboring peoples. North and west of the Great Wall, Shi huangdi's legions defeated the Xiongnu, nomadic, horse-mounted warriors who may have been the same people later known to Europeans as Huns. To the northeast, the prince who ruled Korea acknowledged the Chinese emperor's authority. In the south, the Chinese vanquished the Yueh tribes, overran the territory later included in the southeastern province of Guangxi and Guangdong, and moved into what became Vietnam. The emperor ordered the forced migration of tens of thousands of people into new territories. Some of the settlers were convicts; others were ordinary civilians who were compelled to move and then, as a reward, were exempted for twelve years from the annual period of labor required from imperial subjects as a kind of tax.

The emperor and chancellor Li Si were quick to suppress criticism, especially from scholars who opposed the precepts of legalism. A certain amount of freedom of thought and discourse had been tolerated in the waning decades of the Zhou dynasty, the time of Confucius, but Shi huangdi would have none of it. The past, Li Si declared, must not be used to discredit the present, and thus the past — the books of philosophy and history and poetry written by Zhou sages — had to be destroyed. Countless books laboriously copied on bamboo strips were burned, but enough escaped the purge to preserve China's classics. Even discussing the condemned books was decreed a capital crime. The emperor's own eldest son and heir apparent was exiled to the northern frontier for criticizing his father. And it was said that in the most savage outburst of all, the emperor ordered the execution of 460 scholars, apparently because he suspected they were in league against him.

The First August Sovereign was forty-nine when he died on his last tour of the realm

China's first emperor was only thirteen years old when he ordered work begun on his tomb, but his plans for his afterlife were as grand as his earthly ambitions. For his final dwelling place, Qin Shi Huangdi created in minute detail a subterranean realm over which he expected to rule.

Part of the floor was shaped into a topographical map of the world, in which mercury was made to flow through channels representing the Yellow and Yangtze rivers. Artificial constellations glittered on the ceiling. The tomb was protected by drawn crossbows set to shoot at any intruder whose entry set off their triggers.

But Shi's most spectacular monument lay in four pits to the east of the tomb: a life-size terra-cotta army, more than 6,000 men strong, created to protect him for eternity. The largest of the pits, shown on the following pages, contained the infantry. A second held the cavalry with life-size horses *(below)*, and a third apparently was intended as command headquarters for the still and silent battalions. A fourth pit was empty; the work, begun in 246 BC, was still unfinished when the Qin dynasty fell in 207.

THE ETERNAL ARMY

● INFANTRY
○ ARCHERS
▮ CHARIOTS

Marshaled in columns of four, more than 3,000 terra-cotta foot soldiers *(above)* stand ready to repel any attack on their emperor's tomb. As shown in the diagram at far left, the columns were led by a vanguard of some 200 archers and spearmen, as well as six chariots, each pulled by four horses. The clay warriors were richly detailed, their uniforms and headgear meticulously fashioned according to rank, their clay hair molded into intricate plaits. The artists created the faces without molds, possibly modeling them on actual soldiers. No two are the same, and different ones exhibit the various racial characteristics of the peoples that the emperor united. The figures were brightly painted in colors like those of the kneeling crossbowman at left. These unmoving sentinels were equipped with real weapons — swords and spears and crossbows that would have been lethal in human hands. Some of the emperor's people were not so fortunate as those who posed for the clay figures: A number of his concubines and many slave laborers were buried alive in the tomb.

in 210 BC. The minister Li Si and a eunuch named Zhao Gao who had gained the emperor's confidence immediately hatched a plot. They kept the emperor's death a secret while the caravan bearing his remains returned to the capital; a cartload of fish was pulled behind his closed carriage to hide the odor of his corpse. The dying ruler had written his exiled heir, Prince Fu Su, commanding him to return to the palace. But the plotters intercepted this message and substituted a forged one accusing Fu Su of disloyalty and "permitting" him to commit suicide; the prince obediently complied.

The chancellor and the eunuch were now free to put the late emperor's second son, who was under their control, on the throne. Shi huangdi was laid to rest in a fabulous mausoleum that 700,000 workers had been building throughout most of his reign. There he was surrounded by thousands of life-size terra-cotta soldiers, created by artists to protect him for eternity.

Zhao Gao, the first of a number of notorious eunuchs to play leading roles in Chinese politics, soon outmaneuvered Li Si and in 208 BC arranged his execution: The elderly minister was cut in two at the waist. (Chroniclers left no indications as to how this horrendous but not uncommon punishment was accomplished; it was probably done with a large sword or ax.) Zhao Gao and the new emperor also ordered the deaths of several of the young emperor's brothers and sisters as well as Meng Tian, the engineering genius who had built the Great Wall. Zhao Gao must not have been totally satisfied with his puppet, however, because in 207 BC he staged a mock uprising that induced the emperor to commit suicide. Zhao Gao then placed another young imperial relative on the throne but withheld the title of emperor, declaring him instead to be only a king. This ruler, the third and last in the Qin line, proved as treacherous as his patron. He had the power-hungry eunuch killed, but by now rebellions against the harsh Qin reign were springing to life everywhere.

The two leaders who emerged as the main threats to the throne presented a striking contrast. Xiang Yu was a tall and physically imposing aristocrat who hoped to restore the system of decentralized feudal kingdoms that Shi huangdi had shattered. His rival, Liu Bang, a former minor Qin official who led a force viewed by some as a guerrilla band and by others as a gang of bandits, was a relaxed rustic and a natural leader who gradually attracted more and more followers. In the early stages of the revolts that now flared in several provinces, the two were allies. After Xiang Yu sacked and burned the Qin capital and murdered the young emperor, he and Liu Bang agreed to divide the empire, but the pact soon disintegrated. Xiang Yu at one point offered to settle their differences in one-to-one combat, but Liu preferred to leave the decision to their armies. Xiang set himself up for a short time as the leader of a confederacy of kingdoms in the Zhou style, but Liu finally prevailed. In the climactic clash, Xiang calmly faced Liu's onrushing men and cut his own throat.

The commoner from a central China village was now in unquestioned command. In 202 BC, Liu assumed the throne as the first emperor of the Han dynasty, named for a kingdom he had been granted in his earlier division of China with Xiang Yu. Establishing his capital at Chang'an, later called Xi'an, on the Wei River, he declared a general amnesty and repealed many of the severe laws of his predecessors. Liu broke with Qin practice by naming relatives, favored generals and, generously, a few of his vanquished enemy Xiang's deputies as kings of some of the old provinces. But elsewhere he retained the Qin system of commanderies directly controlled by centralized imperial authority. He had cause to regret reestablishing any kingdoms at all, since he had to put down several revolts led by ungrateful provincial monarchs during his seven-year reign. In 195 BC, he died from an arrow wound suffered in one of those clashes, and the fragility of a succession system complicated by a palace full of imperial consorts was revealed. Theoretically, the emperor designated his successor from among the boys born to his empress and his numerous concubines; the eldest was not automatically chosen. But when Liu died, his widow, the dowager empress Lü, made certain that her son, who was neither the firstborn nor the late emperor's favorite, succeeded him. To accomplish this, she was obliged to do away with both the emperor's designated heir and that prince's concubine mother.

The dowager empress was the real power in the empire until she died fifteen years later, although her son and, after his death, two short-lived sons of his were the nominal rulers. This was the first of several occasions during the Han centuries when imperial wives and their relatives ruled in fact if not in name. Empress Lü ennobled several kinsmen and made a bid to supplant the Liu family with her own, but after her death, Liu's followers regrouped, disposed of the dowager's relations, and placed on the throne another of Liu Bang's sons, who became known as Emperor Wen.

Wen's accession in 180 BC, following the pro forma protestations of reluctance and inadequacy that custom required, was the beginning of an interval of relative peace, stability, prosperity, and expansion of imperial authority. Wen was just what the young empire needed, a gentle and generous sovereign who ruled by Confucian principles, shunning extravagance, soliciting the advice of scholar-statesmen, and — perhaps most suprising of all in the light of China's overall history — easing the plight of the common folk. He eliminated the harsh sanctions for criticizing the government and cut taxes on farm produce. Executions declined, and no more books were burned. Wen and his successors carved the provincial kingdoms into smaller and smaller states while extending and consolidating imperial control. By the time an emperor named Wu Di came to the throne in 140 BC, the empire contained forty directly controlled commanderies and twenty-five small kingdoms, the latter the enfeebled remnants of the warring states that had once contested for mastery of all China.

Wu Di, meaning "the martial emperor," was one of the most successful rulers China ever had. He was something of a mystic and a lover of regal luxury whose gardens were rife with exotic fauna and flora — orchids and sweetly scented cassia trees, gaudy peacocks and screeching monkeys, kingfishers and pheasants. But Wu was no dilettante. During his long and fruitful reign, from 140 to 87 BC, he gathered still more power to the central government, stabilized the economy by introducing copper coins, and raised the quality of the civil service by seeking highly qualified candidates and initiating competitive tests. And under his leadership, Han military might and expansionism reached its peak. China was rich and stable enough now to mount both military and commercial expeditions into the world beyond the Wall.

The Xiongnu nomads of the north, whose sporadic raids had persisted despite the Great Wall and a series of diplomatic overtures, were the chief object of Wu's military attention. The Chinese had been puzzled to discover that the material niceties they could offer meant nothing to the loutish Xiongnu. "They have no desire for our things," a diplomat complained. They preferred their crude clothing of animal hides to the silk the Chinese sent them. Because force seemed to be the only language they understood, Wu went after them with huge armies numbering as many as 100,000 cavalrymen supported by infantry and other troops. The Han armies included volunteers and convicts, but most of the soldiers were conscripts called up for two-year periods of service. All males between twenty-three and fifty-six years of age who were not exempt for some special reason were drafted, although buying a substitute was permitted. Wu's well-organized legions never conclusively subdued the Xiongnu but did push deep into their territory in a series of fierce battles. The Han consolidated their gains by erecting a 300-mile western extension of the Great Wall.

Wu's soldiers also recaptured large expanses of territory south of the Yangtze Valley that had thrown off the Chinese imperial yoke since the fall of the Qin, including part of Annam, later called Vietnam. In the northeast, Han armies conquered sections of Manchuria and Korea, establishing a colony in Korea that would remain a Chinese outpost for the next four centuries. By 119 BC, Wu's aggressive imperialism had added eighteen new commanderies to China, many of them peopled by non-Chinese.

A strategy conceived during the campaign against the Xiongnu led to a mission that became one of the legendary epics of ancient China. Wu wanted to make contact with a semicivilized people called the Yuezhi, who had been driven far out onto the western steppes by the Xiongnu. His idea was an alliance that would catch the Xiongnu in a pincer, easing the pressure on his empire. But first someone had to find

the Yuezhi. A gentleman of the Han court named Zhang Qian volunteered to try, and in 138 BC he set out westward with a party of about a hundred.

The rub was that Zhang had to cross Xiongnu territory. He and his men were captured almost immediately, and Zhang spent the next ten years as a prisoner. He eventually escaped and doggedly carried on, trekking west with the survivors of the original band until he finally came upon the Yuezhi in Bactria, north and east of Iran.

A tomb relief *(above)* of the goddess Xiwangmu, who ruled eternal paradise, the jade burial suit of Princess Tou Wan, and the poem by Cao Zhi illustrate the Han concern with immortality. Those who could not afford complete suits like the princess's, in which 2,156 jade pieces were joined by gold thread, used jade as plugs for the body and as covers for the eyes and tongue. Jade was believed — erroneously — to preserve the body.

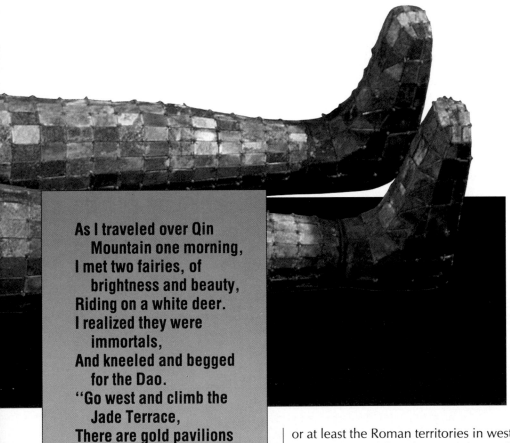

As I traveled over Qin
   Mountain one morning,
I met two fairies, of
   brightness and beauty,
Riding on a white deer.
I realized they were
   immortals,
And kneeled and begged
   for the Dao.
"Go west and climb the
   Jade Terrace,
There are gold pavilions
   and corridors."
They gave me an immortal
   elixir.
"Your longevity will
   match that of gold and
   jade,
And you will never reach
   senility."

The Yuezhi, to Zhang's dismay, were content where they were and had no desire to resume combat with the Xiongnu, so the mission was a failure. Zhang took a southerly route back to avoid the barbarians, but he was captured again anyway and held for another year. Twelve years after he had marched off, he reappeared at the Han capital of Chang'an with a Xiongnu wife and one survivor from his original party.

He brought home no alliance, but he did bring animal and plant specimens, reportedly including cultivated grapes, and wondrous tales: of people who rode elephants, of lands of great wealth, and of a kingdom called Ferghana where Chinese silk might be traded for swift and stately horses. Zhang's hard-won report led to the establishment of the Silk Road, the great trade corridor across western China and central Asia that would for the first time link the land of Confucius with the West.

Trade caravans soon began to clatter west through the panhandle between Tibet's mountains and the northern deserts, then on past the cities later called Tashkent and Samarkand to Parthia, where Chinese goods were traded to Iranians who carried them to the Mediterranean. Silk was the most coveted Chinese export borne along the routes in this corridor. Trade missions sponsored by the government exported silk both in its raw form and as finished cloth. Caravans also carried gold, cinnamon, and skins, and they returned home with wine, spices, linen, horses, woolen goods, and such exotic food plants as pomegranates, broad beans, and sesame.

A number of previously independent states and tribes along the Silk Road became in effect subjects of the Chinese during the next 300 years. They paid tribute to the Han overlord with goods and provided hostages, often the sons of rulers, as earnests of their continued fealty. Hostages from no fewer than fifty tributary states would be living in China by AD 174, some of them studying at Chinese schools and bearing Chinese titles giving them privileged status. China's military posture dovetailed with its trade policy: Detachments of soldiers were posted at various sites along the silk route to fend off persistently marauding warrior tribes, and the government barred export of such strategic items as weapons and iron goods.

The Chinese became aware of Rome — or at least the Roman territories in western Asia — through their dealings at the western terminus of the Chinese section of the Silk Road. Parthia discouraged any direct contact between Rome and China, in order to protect its profitable role as the middleman. One Han envoy who was bound for the land that the Chinese called Da Qin — the eastern Roman Empire — was halted at the shore of the Persian Gulf by Parthians, who dissuaded him from proceeding farther by convincing him that the voyage could take two years and that there was "something in the sea which made men homesick."

The Chinese who traveled to Parthia marveled at a country where silver coins circulated and the people made "signs on leather by way of literary record." Roman merchants and perhaps Greeks as well probably mixed with Chinese in the Parthian markets. The earliest recorded official contact between Chinese and Romans was a visit to the Han court in AD 166 by men who said they were emissaries of "Andun, king of Da Qin," believed to be the Roman emperor Marcus Aurelius Antoninus. A Chinese chronicler said the Romans brought gifts of ivory, rhinoceros horn, and tortoiseshell.

There were other avenues to the outer world. On his long travels, Zhang Qian had heard of a southerly trade corridor from the province of Sichuan to India by way of Burma. The Chinese explored the route, and official relations between the two greatest civilizations of ancient Asia were established no later than the first century AD. Indians brought tribute to the Chinese court late in that century, and the Indians may also have relayed Chinese silk to Rome by sea. China also established commercial relations during this period with Japan, still a land of simple tribal villages.

The cost of the venturesome military and commercial initiatives launched during Emperor Wu's fifty-three-year reign forced the government to find new sources of income. China's revenue came primarily from the peasant farmers, who were obliged to contribute to the imperial government one-fifteenth of the produce from their small, intensively worked plots. (They often were squeezed for much more than that by officials lining their own pockets.) Another tax was assessed on each individual, the rate varying with the taxpayer's age, sex, and place of residence. Although most farmers barely got by, they were recognized in offical rhetoric and to some degree in practice as the empire's backbone. Thus, when imperial expenditures overtook income, the regime sought other remedies instead of dunning the peasants for higher taxes. One solution was nationalizing the iron and salt industries, which until Wu's time had been in private hands. The government also sold military titles, introduced fines for criminal offenses, boosted taxes on merchants — an officially disparaged but often prosperous class — and squeezed the nobility for special levies. The imperial treasury was further fattened by rent on state land leased to tenant farmers.

In addition to bearing the expense of armies and trade missions, the government built new roads in the south and southwest and added to the maze of canals that functioned as the main routes for grain transport. Labor on public-works projects such as roads, walls, and royal tombs was partially provided by men drafted for one month of obligatory, unpaid service each year. Criminals, as well, worked in forced-labor gangs. The state also concerned itself with the operation of the economy as a whole, trying to smooth market fluctuations by buying staple crops when they were cheap and selling them when prices rose.

On paper, Han government was tidy. The administrative levels were stacked in a neat pyramid — from a base of hamlets, each composed of a single clan or a few families, to communes and districts, then to county-sized prefectures and on to state-sized commanderies, and finally to the ultimate authority that rested with the emperor and his cabinet. A triumvirate of imperial advisers stood just below the emperor — the chancellor, who was in charge of finance; an imperial counselor, who headed the bureaucracy (130,000 strong around AD 1); and the commander in chief of the armed forces. Nine cabinet-level ministers on the next rung down had responsibilities ranging from the imperial purse to the royal stables; one minister's territory embraced "religious ceremonies, observation of the stars, and record keeping."

In practice, of course, it was not quite so neat. The commanderies or provinces, for example (there were eighty-three by the end of the dynasty), were administered by governors named and controlled by the emperor. But there were also twenty kingdoms in that same period, although they were actually ruled by imperially appointed officials rather than by their nominal hereditary monarchs. And as time passed, an "inner court" of unofficial but influential advisers grew up around the emperor, occasionally including eunuchs who were theoretically only "palace attendants."

Still, most Han governments made a formal effort to enlist as officials the finest men available. During Wu's reign, senior officials were told to nominate as civil-service candidates young men of high intelligence and integrity. Eventually, a quota specified one candidate for bureaucratic training for every 200,000 citizens. They were given examinations, hired on a year's probation, and then subjected to performance reviews every three years. The exams tested their understanding of classic works attributed to Confucius — material that would remain the basis of Chinese civil-service examinations into the early years of the twentieth century AD. The competitive recruiting system, admirable in so many respects, was not absolutely airtight. Family connections were helpful. Officials could nominate their sons or their friends' sons, and the relatives of favored imperial concubines often found the path to advancement smoothed for them. For those who patiently rose through the ranks, the rewards were great: generous salaries (twenty times higher for the top grades than the bottom), exemption from military and labor service, one day off out of every five, and sometimes even a pension. To forestall corruption, an official was not permitted to serve in his home district.

The richly patterned swatch of fabric below bears testimony to the skills of Han China's silk weavers. They created their exquisite products with machines such as the treadle loom *(inset),* which was used in China centuries before it appeared in the West. Chinese silk fabrics with their extremely complicated designs were an important commodity at home as well as abroad. In China, the wealthy dressed in silk finery, and bolts of silk were often used as a medium of exchange.

Bureaucrats spent their days collecting taxes, supervising the maintenance of roads, seeing to the delivery of mail by runners or mounted couriers, administering the laws of the land, and writing reports. There were 1,587 prefectures in AD 2, each with a walled-town county seat where masses of records piled up, most written on narrow strips of bamboo fastened together with hemp tapes (silk was used instead of wood for diagrams, maps, and documents that required a special elegance). A poet of the era captured the daily round: "Office work, a wearisome jumble; / ink drafts, a cross-hatch of deletions and smears; / racing the writing brush, no time to eat, / sun slanting down but never a break; / swamped and muddled in records and reports, / head spinning till it's senseless and numb."

The laws enforced by Han officials forbade — along with such crimes as murder, robbery, and bribery — a host of offenses against his imperial majesty, including reviling the emperor. Suspects were sometimes beaten during interrogation, but they did receive a trial in which charges were read and witnesses heard. In capital cases, death was imposed by beheading. For the most extreme offenses, a felon's family was also executed. Conviction for lesser crimes could mean mutilation by tattooing, amputation of nose or feet, or castration. The most common punishment was hard labor for one to five years. Sometimes petty offenders got off with mere fines.

The Han Chinese world view was remarkably homogeneous for such a populous and huge nation. The Chinese believed that the earth comprised nine continents separated by water, and that each continent was further divided into nine regions; China was merely one region of one continent. The Chinese name for the Roman territories in western Asia, Da Qin (Great Qin), suggests that they recognized Rome as a comparable power. Nonetheless, the Han Chinese adhered to their ancestors' conviction that theirs was the middle or central kingdom, surrounded by concentric rings of territory occupied successively by loyalists and subject peoples and finally the barbarians of the outer ring.

Confucianism dominated the philosophical, ethical, and political thought of the Han rulers. Emperor Wu was following Confucian precepts when he established a system of examinations to recruit the brightest provincial youths for government service. Confucianism emphasized learning, harmony, moderation, tolerance, courtesy, and respect for the past. Its central, untranslatable doctrine of *li* connoted proper conduct in all matters, great and small; it was the right way to behave, to believe, and to rule. In the second century AD, the Confucian classics were carved in stone in the Han capital, and pilgrims journeyed from distant provinces to gaze upon them and copy the words of these definitive versions of the great thinker's ideas.

The Han version of Confucianism was a pragmatic interpretation that accommodated or coexisted with other systems of thought. Legalism, for example — the belief in a strong and harsh government — was seen as fitting within a Confucian framework, although it had to sacrifice some of its intemperate emphasis on discipline and punishment. The Confucian ideal of rationality and balance left little room for superstition and spiritualism, but cults devoted to such practices

A Han ritual hall such as this one, known as a Ming-tang, was used as an academy, as a celestial observatory and, most important, as a temple. On the first level, young men destined for imperial service received an education based on the Confucian classics. From the top floor, astronomers studied the heavens. On the middle level, as shown in the diagram above the building, religious ceremonies were performed. Both numerology and astrology dictated the floor's design. Altogether there were nine rooms. The eight outer rooms had a total of twelve outer walls, which represented the twelve new moons in a year. The central hall, plus the four corner chambers, represented the five elements: earth *(at the center)*, wood, fire, metal, and water. The remaining four rooms were to symbolize the four seasons of the year, based on the directions they faced: north, winter; south, summer; east, spring; west, autumn. Each was also identified with a particular color and deity. When the emperor worshiped in a Ming-tang, he changed rooms, robes, and rituals with the seasons. Eaves tiles along the four sides depicted the beasts associated with the four quarters of heaven: the green dragon on the east, the white tiger facing west, the red bird to the south, and the black tortoise on the north.

WINTER

AUTUMN

SPRING

SUMMER

flourished in Han society. Even Daoism, with its aloofness from worldly concerns and its emphasis on individualism and spontaneity, had adherents among the ruling families. Confucian teachings were flexible enough that they could comfortably embrace such seemingly incompatible ideas.

The prevailing religion, like the Confucian ethical system, was an amalgam of beliefs that had persisted from earliest times or evolved in the preceding centuries. People honored their ancestors. They placated evil spirits with animal sacrifices. They worshiped nature. They equated the state with the divine order, and they explained the cycles of life, death, and the seasons in terms of fundamental forces they called yin and yang. Yin — cool, dark, female, submissive — alternated in ascendancy with warm, bright, male, aggressive yang. Yin was winter, yang was summer. Some animals were yin (camels, for example) and others yang (horses). All phenomena fell into one category or the other, and the interplay between them influenced everything. The elements the Chinese called "the five cosmic forces" — water, fire, metal, wood, and earth — were also highly significant. The dynamics among the five, the shifting preeminence of one or another of them, accounted for the flow of human events. The five were associated with distinct colors and directions (the four compass points plus the earth in the center) and different dynasties: The Han was fire, and its color was red.

The emperor had a religious duty to keep his realm in harmony with heaven and earth and the deities that ruled them. If he failed, the consequences for his people were famines, floods, and earthquakes. To fulfill this obligation, the Son of Heaven regularly trekked to five sacred mountains, located in the uplands that surrounded the Yellow River plain. Among those peaks, he sought divine blessings for his domain through prayer and sacrifices. Emperors also offered prayers to the gods and goddesses of earth, sun, rain, and rivers and sought guidance from the spirits of their ancestors. The belief in an elixir of immortality, which had led the Qin emperor Shi huangdi to send an armada full of young people to unknown islands in the eastern sea, persisted among many educated Chinese, as did the notion that lesser metals could be transmuted into gold. Many people trusted in sorcerers, magic rites, and mystic intermediaries with the beyond. Buddhist traders and missionaries from India appeared in China in the first century AD and soon began establishing shrines and centers, but Buddhism would not gain a firm foothold in China until after the fall of the Han.

Han society was a carefully delineated hierarchy, with gradations deriving from heredity, professional position, education, and other factors. Mental work was more highly esteemed than physical effort or moneymaking in the Confucian value scheme — hence the importance of education — and political power carried more prestige than wealth did. Among commoners, scholars ranked highest, followed by farmers, artisans, and merchants, in that order.

It was possible to cross the social barriers. The first Han emperor, Liu Bang, a man of humble village origins, is the best example, but many talented individuals rose from rude beginnings to high office and even into the hereditary nobility, primarily by way of scholarship and the civil service. A man named Gongsun Hong was celebrated for ascending from swineherd to chancellor. Consort families, with no qualifications other than a daughter who happened to catch the imperial eye, could climb to power and riches with breathtaking speed and plunge to disgrace just as precipitously.

The atmosphere at the top of the Han social pyramid was rarefied indeed. The emperor was a figure of such remote grandeur that people were forbidden to speak or write his name. Even ministers were not allowed to address him directly; they instead

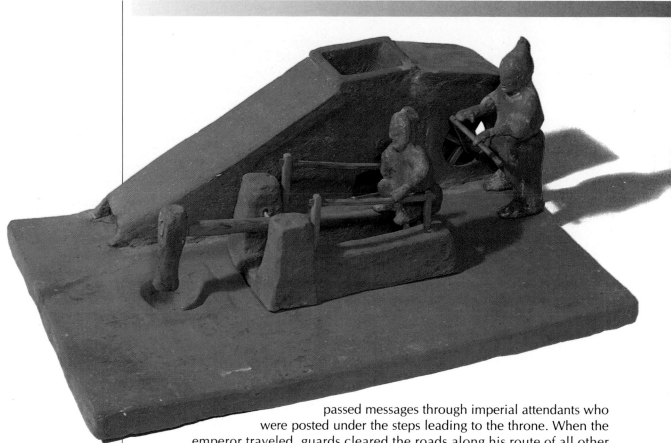

Agricultural workers use ingenious machines to clean rice in this earthenware model found in a Han tomb. The squatting figure works a huller with a treadle-operated tilt hammer, the earliest known anywhere, to smash the shells of the grain. The rice is then funneled into the top of the winnower, where a fan — powered by a crank turned by the second figure — blows away the hull debris. The cleaned rice pours out through the opening in front. The Chinese apparently used the crank several centuries before the device was known in Europe.

passed messages through imperial attendants who were posted under the steps leading to the throne. When the emperor traveled, guards cleared the roads along his route of all other traffic. He rode in gilded carriages unlike any others and dressed in robes that signified his eminence. Ignoring palace protocol could be fatal: Intruders were summarily killed, a nobleman who cursed the emperor was cleaved in two, and another who sullied the court's dignity by getting drunk and singing was encouraged to commit suicide. Theoretically the emperor could do away with anyone for any reason whatever; Wu, obeying an imperative connected with some superstition, once ordered the execution of everyone in the imperial prison.

New women for the emperor's harem were recruited in the eighth month of each year by palace officials who selected from among teenaged virgins only, on the basis of beauty, elegance of manner, and respectability. The imperial concubines, who numbered in the thousands during Wu's reign, were divided into fourteen ranks corresponding to civil-service categories. (Those of the top rank were titled brilliant companions.) Later the fourteen ranks were compressed to three: honorable lady, beautiful lady, and chosen lady. The emperor's principal wife, who became empress, came from among the concubines, and thus often started life as a commoner. A harem was a sign of status; many nobles, high-level officials, and wealthy merchants had them, but monogamy was the rule among ordinary citizens. Girls from poor families were sometimes sold or abducted into service as concubines.

High officials and nobles were expected to dress and travel in keeping with their rank. The emperor could bestow twenty orders of privilege for merit, the top twelve limited to government officials. A holder of the highest of these outranked everyone save the emperor and his immediate family and was entitled to collect taxes from households in the territory allotted to him. Many lower-ranking nobles enjoyed prosperous lives on self-sufficient estates where their needs were served by dozens of men and women. Even a farm owned by an army colonel, a figure of no great status, included its own brewery — in addition to vegetable gardens, livestock, a mulberry grove for silkworm cultivation, and pools in which hemp was soaked as a preliminary step in processing the fiber.

Peasant farmers, who constituted perhaps 90 percent of the population, had a much harsher existence. They had to toil endlessly to stay ahead of their creditors and the tax collector. "Farmers plow in spring, weed in summer, reap in autumn, and store in winter," a contemporary chronicler wrote. "They cut undergrowth and wood for fuel and render labor services to the government. All year round they cannot afford to take even a day's rest." To pay taxes "farmers have to sell their possessions at half price, and those who are destitute have to borrow money at 200 percent interest. Eventually they have to sell fields and dwellings, or sometimes sell even children and grandchildren into slavery in order to pay back the loan."

Farmers commonly grew grain crops — wheat, millet, barley in the north, rice in the south — on meager family plots that averaged no more than about eleven acres. Records for one village showed that 105 people coaxed a living out of twenty-five farms averaging a little more than three acres each. They used ox-drawn plows and iron tools and alternated the furrows and the intervening ridges annually, because they did not have enough land to leave a whole field fallow for a year. Some more fortunate farmers supplemented their staple crops by growing hemp for rope and textile fiber; bamboo for construction use, writing material, water pipes, chopsticks, and other purposes; and fruit such as peaches, plums, and melons. Silk cultivation, which required mulberry orchards to feed the worms, expanded during the Han period from the center of the country around the Yellow River region outward to the frontier provinces.

Probably 10 percent of the Chinese lived in some 1,500 towns that ranged in size from a few hundred inhabitants up to the 300,000 to 650,000 of Chang'an, perhaps the largest metropolis on earth. That splendid imperial capital, with its handsome gates, 150-foot-wide boulevards, and lush royal parks, was built at the beginning of the Han era, apparently by some 150,000 conscripted peasants. The city was surrounded by a seventeen-foot-high wall and divided into 160 wards by other walls, presumably to facilitate control of the populace. Spectacular palaces and mansions adjoined the imperial gardens, which held ornamental towers, manmade lakes, and exotic beasts. There was a "hall of brilliance" for state religious ceremonies and several shrines honoring the imperial ancestors.

Residents shopped at nine walled markets scattered throughout the city. Market stalls were grouped by the products they sold: lacquerware vendors in one area, sellers of pelts and hides in another, stalls offering brass, cloth, food, cinnabar, and even carriages, each among similar neighbors. Merchants, officially deemed parasites who fed off the honorable farmers, prospered — as did grain brokers, manufacturers, and money-lenders. Han law persecuted merchants, barring them from holding office, owning land, or riding horses, but that usually did not hurt their livelihoods. Big businessmen, the truly wealthy ones, sometimes bribed officials to escape registration as merchants and thus avoided the stigma. An official at the court of Emperor Wen wrote that "merchants are rich and honored though they are humbled by the law; farmers are poor and lowly though they are respected by the law."

Most factories were located in cities. The manufacture of metalware and craft goods

In a flurry of culinary activity depicted in the kitchen scene below, servants stoke the stove, knead dough, and prepare a fish while an animal — presumably another course — is dragged into the room. At right, a servant, or possibly a merchant, cleans a fish, with a pail beneath the table for slops. The figure and the bas-relief both came from Han tombs, whose occupants liked to be buried among depictions of ordinary life.

was primarily under government auspices and tight bureaucratic management, with banks of supervisors assigned to oversee the production of iron tools and weapons, bronzeware, lacquered goods, funerary objects, and other manufactured products. The lucrative salt and iron industries that became state monopolies in the early years of the Han dynasty later reverted to private ownership. Brewing and textile production were among many small-scale businesses run by private enterprise.

Earlier Chinese iron makers had shaped iron into tools, weapons, and other objects by hammering it while it was red hot. In this era, foundry workers learned to pour molten iron into clay molds to cool — evidently the first time the cast-iron process was used anywhere. By heating cast iron until most of the carbon was gone, they produced steel, which they called "great iron." When virtually all the carbon was removed, they got wrought iron; the Chinese called it "ripe iron."

Skilled artisans took great pride in their work. Lacquerware from one government workshop was inscribed with the name of every person who had anything to do with making it, including no less than six foremen and supervisors who may never have touched a tool. The identities and job description of the artisans could still be read almost 2,000 years later — Li and Jie the lacquer applicators, Zhang who gilded the bronze handles, Fang the painter, Guang who did the final cleansing and inspection.

Manufacturers sometimes inscribed more general messages on their wares. They decorated roof tiles with such hopeful homilies as "Profound happiness without an end" and "Long life without limit." Engravings on some privately made bronze mirrors were essentially early advertisements. "The mirrors made by the Ye family are handsome and great," one declared. "They are as bright as the sun and moon." Another claimed that its buyer "will live long and continue to enjoy wealth and prestige."

Slaves ranked lowest on the social scale. Slavery was not essential to the economy of Han China as it was to that of contemporary Rome. Slaves never made up more than 1 percent of the population, and they had more to do with enhancing the status of their owners than with supplying crucial labor. Families of convicted criminals were sometimes condemned to slavery; the poor sold themselves or their children into bondage; and prisoners of war were often enslaved. The regime meted out slaves as rewards to faithful officials, and some landowners kidnapped peasants and forced them into servitude. Slaves were sold at pens in urban markets, along with horses and cattle. Babies born to female slaves were committed to a life of servitude.

Slaves functioned for the most part as household servants and ornaments for the wealthy, although some worked in fields and mines and even craft shops. The more gifted among them were trained to amuse the elite as musicians and acrobats. Red-kerchiefed slaves did the cooking and serving at the imperial palace, where they also worked as messengers, doorkeepers, and bodyguards.

The family was the frame and focus of life in Han China — not the multigenerational "extended" family that was to flourish later in China but the nucleus of father, mother, and children. (Han law actively discouraged extended families by imposing double taxes on households that included two or more grown sons; no clue was left as to the purpose of the law, but its effect was to force many adult males from their parents' homes.) Family loyalty, obedience, and mutual dependence were central to the Chinese character; the family functioned as a largely self-sufficient economic unit, a repository of religious tradition, and a cheering section. The success or failure of one member affected the others, and they shared the spoils of a promotion or the shame of an arrest. Soldiers on garrison duty at the Great Wall brought their families with them.

Fathers were in charge and punished their adult sons as if they were still children. But the position of women in Han society was strikingly different from what it was to become in later periods. Women could inherit property and continue to own it after they married. They commonly remarried, either after leaving their husbands or after their husbands had died. This notable freedom of women existed in spite of Confucian admonitions to the contrary. A book called *Lessons for Women* spelled out the Confucian notion of the female's ideal attitude: "to be modest, yielding, and respectful, to put others first and herself last, to bear disgrace and humiliation, and always to have a feeling of fear. . . . Strength is the glory of men, weakness is women's good quality." Practicing medicine was one of the few occupations open to women.

Grain-based dishes like wheat or millet cakes were likely to be on the table when the members of a peasant family picked up their chopsticks and ate, possibly supplemented by home-grown vegetables such as beans or turnips and perhaps fruit for dessert. A well-paid bureaucrat might have pork and chicken fairly regularly, washed down with beer or rice wine. Vendors in Chang'an's markets sold cooked meat, syrups, dried fish, relishes, and pickled foods to those who could afford them. China's subtropical southern provinces also produced oranges, tangerines, and coconuts.

For most people the family home was a rectangular wooden house, with plastered interior walls, set in the middle of a walled courtyard. A garden and various outbuildings normally adjoined the house. Stone was reserved for tombs and religious buildings, and the walls of public structures were often decorated with colorful murals depicting scenes from China's already-long history.

Dress differed with status. The upper classes wore silk outfits and cloth slippers, although leather was also popular. Peasants dressed in hemp tunics and straw sandals. Wealthy women used rouge and rice powder, and drew eyebrow lines that followed fashion's swings — arrowlike points during one period, gentle arches in another.

Chinese life was full of entertainment at every level of society. Everyone enjoyed music and dancing, the elite at lavish private concerts where five-piece orchestras performed, and the common folk at seasonal festivals and funerals. Musicians played the traditional drums, bells, and flutes along with harps and lutes brought back from western Asia by wayfaring Chinese. Confucius had taught that music had powers to elevate or degrade the spirit, and music was thus treated as a serious matter requiring the attention of a government bureau, the office of music. This lively agency was staffed at one point by 829 singers and instrumentalists, but it was abolished late in the first century BC when it was decided that concerts too often aroused base and unseemly passions, just as Confucius had feared they might.

The well-to-do also enjoyed tiger fights, performing animals, and exhibitions of juggling, acrobatics, and swordplay, while the sandal-clad crowd gathered at cockfights and horse races. And there were simpler entertainments for idle hours at home: In a board game called Liubo, players shook dicelike marked bamboo sticks out of a cup to determine where they moved a counter on the board.

The education system in Han China was probably the most advanced on earth at the time, even though the sole purpose of school was to transform promising boys, most of them from the upper strata of society, into learned and upright government officials. They studied at the huge imperial academy, where enrollment at one point topped 30,000, or in private seminaries run by scholars. Students learned to write, studied the Confucian classics and scriptural texts, and puzzled out mathematics problems of a sort that would change very little over the next 2,000 years: "If a man is paid forty coins for carrying two measures of salt for a distance of 100 *li*, how much will he be paid for carrying 1.73 measures for a distance of 80 *li?* '' At graduation they got first-, second-, and third-class degrees. Educated gentlemen sometimes expressed themselves in poetry of a pronounced melancholy cast, one of the more admired modes: ''Green green the cypress on the ridge, / Stones heaped about in mountain streams; / Between heaven and earth our lives rush past / Like travelers with a long road to go. . . . / Man lives out his little sojourn, / Scudding by like a swirl of dust. . . .''

Although Chinese attainments in the plastic arts (especially bronze and lacquerware) and in music and literature were impressive, it was in science and technology that this brilliant civilization's achievements were most dazzling. Chinese astronomers were the most advanced of their time. They watched the heavens through bronze tubes fitted with a special device they invented that divided the sky into measured segments. They were the first to understand that sunspots were features of the sun's surface and not objects in space, and in the fourth century BC they fixed the length of the solar year at 365¼ days by studying the stars. Their records of eclipses and comet sightings, which they regarded as omens, were the most systematic and exhaustive in the ancient world. Their descriptions in 240 BC of what would later be called Halley's comet were to survive as the earliest known accounts of that intriguing heavenly body.

Chinese physicians were specializing in fields such as nutrition and internal medicine as early as the third century BC. They recognized the cause of vitamin-deficiency diseases, even though they did not identify vitamins as such, and prescribed effective remedies. They dispensed therapeutic herbs that would still be used in the twentieth

Ancient Innovations

The emergence of empires brought a rare measure of stability to the ancient world and created a climate for technological advances. From Europe to the Far East, great thinkers and tinkerers alike produced a raft of inventions, improvements, and gadgetry. The practical-minded Chinese, emphasizing utility, compiled a long list of important inventions: paper, the wheelbarrow, the suspension bridge, the stirrup, and the magic lantern — the forerunner of movies. The Romans turned their minds to engineering and built roads, aqueducts, baths, and sewers. And the Greeks, brilliant theorists who scorned experimentation involving manual labor, devised ingenious mechanical gimmicks that were based on sophisticated physical principles.

At the same time, inventors in different cultures came independently to similar ideas, and technological innovations developed in one empire were advanced in another. The water pump, devised by an Alexandrian named Ctesibius, was modified by a countryman named Hero. Chang Heng, a royal astronomer in Han China, invented a seismograph *(below)* that recorded earthquakes by dropping balls — a method also used by Hero in an odometer, to measure distance. The Romans had another idea for an odometer, one based on a system of gears.

A Chinese seismograph, invented in AD 132, signaled an earthquake and indicated its direction through the release of a bronze ball that dropped from the mouth of a dragon into the mouth of a toad below. Inside the jar, an inverted pendulum tilted when the earth trembled, falling into one of eight channels facing different ways. As it moved, it pushed a trigger that opened the dragon's jaws and expelled the ball.

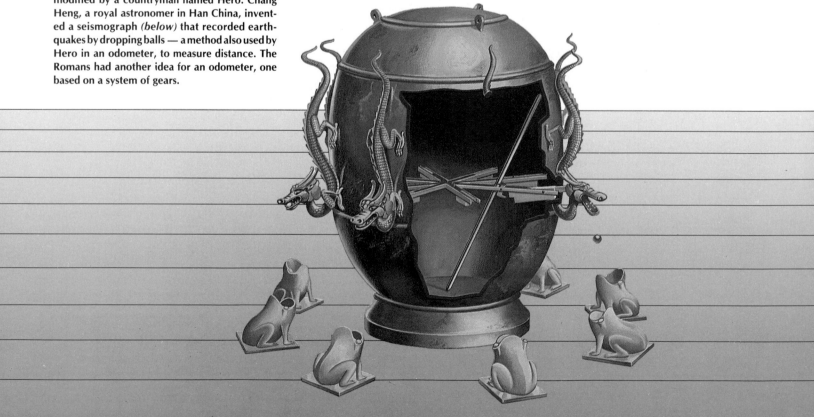

century AD. Veterinarians were practicing their healing arts in the same period.

Inventive tinkerers flourished in Han China. Chinese artisans were the first to hit on the idea of making paper, pounding hemp, tree bark, or rags into pulp and coating the resultant sediment with gelatin. The invention of paper would be officially attributed to a man named Cai Lun in AD 105, but it probably was being made at least 200 years earlier. Although it eventually preempted wood and silk as a writing material, paper was apparently first used for wrapping and clothing.

Chinese technological virtuosity surfaced in many other inventions and processes. A many-sided genius named Zhang Heng devised the world's first seismograph in earthquake-prone China in AD 132. Salt miners, using iron drill bits driven by men jumping onto seesawlike levers, drilled 4,800-foot-deep boreholes to extract salt from the earth. Miners also discovered natural gas in what they called "fire wells" and channeled it through pipes to outlets where it was used as fuel. Han Chinese built the first suspension bridge and developed a lodestone compass they called a "south pointer" with a spoon-shaped needle. One Ge You was credited with introducing an implement — the wheelbarrow — that became indispensable on construction sites in the first century BC, more than a thousand years before Europeans devised one.

The decades that followed the death of Emperor Wu, by natural causes in 87 BC, were a time of military and economic retrenchment and gradual decline of the dynasty. Under a series of weak or dissipated rulers, the Han court deteriorated into chronic palace intrigues and factional struggles. By the last decade of the first century BC, the dynasty was staggering, and China's influence beyond its borders was minimal. Politi-

A precursor of today's vending machines, this invention of Hero's dispensed sacred water in which Greeks washed their hands before performing sacrifices. A coin was dropped through the slot in the lid and fell onto the round plate below. The weight of the coin pushed the plate down and opened a valve, releasing a dollop of the liquid. Many of Hero's clever inventions were designed, as this one was, for use in temples and theaters.

A model of a technological breakthrough, this device has been called Hero's steam engine. A hollow ball was suspended between two pipes, over a closed caldron of water. When a fire caused the water to boil, steam passed up one of the pipes and into the ball. The steam escaped through two jets, placed opposite each other so that the pressure caused the ball to rotate — potentially at very high speeds.

cal power had accrued to a family named Wang, whose influence began when a royal concubine from that clan bore a son who became emperor, elevating his mother to the position of dowager empress. The most gifted and ambitious of the Wangs was a nephew of the dowager, Wang Mang. He was a scholarly Confucian of temperate habits who became a fascinating and enigmatic figure on China's political stage. Named regent for the eight-year-old Han ruler in AD 1, Wang became acting emperor when the boy died. He was succeeded by an infant prince four years later. Soon afterward, however, reports of auspicious omens signifying a dynastic change mysteriously began circulating — dreams of heavenly intervention, the discovery of an ox turned to stone. In AD 9, Wang Mang yielded to the inevitable and declared himself the first emperor of a dynasty designated Xin, or ''New.''

Wang Mang promptly launched a program of dramatic reforms addressing injustices that had been mounting for decades. He decreed a breakup of the large estates, redistributing the land to the peasantry. He declared an end to slavery and prohibited the sale of either land or slaves. He tried to stabilize prices and protect farmers from price-gouging merchants. He offered low-interest government loans for various enterprises, demoted the Han nobles to commoners, and even cut bureaucratic salaries. To reduce the economic power of the wealthy and to enrich the imperial purse, he ordered that all privately held gold be turned in to the treasury in exchange for bronze. Not surprisingly, he alienated almost everyone with any power.

Under pressure from the moneyed class, he was forced to repeal the laws against slavery and land purchases three years later, but it was nature and not the nobles that

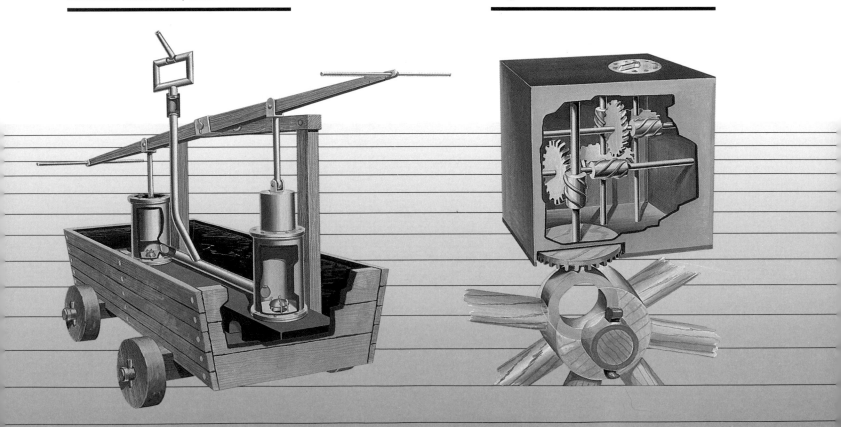

The prolific inventor Hero devised this water pump, which was used to put out fires. The pump, submerged in a water tank on wheels, was powered by men stationed at each end of a rocker arm. The seesaw motion of the rocker arm operated a system of valves and pistons that drew water into two bronze cylinders. When a piston was pushed down, the water was forced through a one-way flap valve, into a T-shaped pipe, and out a nozzle that could be swiveled in any direction.

This odometer, used by ancient surveyors to measure distance traveled, was a predecessor of the modern taxi meter. A peg on the hub of a wagon wheel was connected to a set of reduction gears in a box on the vehicle. For each revolution of the wheel, the first gear moved one tooth, and for each complete revolution of the first gear, the second moved one tooth. Odometers usually had five or more such gears, the smallest of them connected to a graduated dial that showed distance traveled.

eventually precipitated his downfall. Two catastrophic floods within eight years dev-astated the Yellow River plain, drowning thousands and turning millions more into starving refugees. The homeless peasants united in bandit gangs that pillaged the countryside, eventually forming an organized movement known as the "Red Eye-brows" for the paint they daubed on their foreheads. By AD 18 the Red Eyebrow uprising had become a full-scale rebellion. Wang Mang mobilized an army that stalled their momentum, but he failed to subdue them. The always-opportunistic Xiongnu saw an opening and invaded the northwestern territory where the Old Silk Road ran.

After several years of bloody civil war, the scales tilted against the regime when the leaders of the Liu family, descendants of the Han emperors, allied themselves with the rebels. In AD 23 the united Han and Red Eyebrow armies marched on Chang'an, collecting mobs of civilians on the way. They broke through a gate in the east wall and besieged the palace. Wang Mang's guards hustled the emperor to a part of the com-pound called Terrace Bathed by Water, where the invading soldiers found him. They decapitated him on the spot. Millions had died as the result of floods, starvation, and warfare, and the Chinese nation was exhausted. Wang Mang's great experiment had failed, and the Han were once again supreme.

Guangwu Di, the first ruler of the Han restoration, steered the empire through the stormy aftermath of the rebellion and revived China's flagging fortunes. He moved the imperial court from burned and plundered Chang'an eastward to Luoyang, which long before had been the seat of the Zhou dynasty. Guangwu Di was a strong leader and, like his predecessor, a disciple of Confucius. He and his successors gradually reestab-lished Chinese control over the country infiltrated by the Xiongnu. The wall once again defined the border. Guangwu restored the Han administrative system and reinstated the imperial prerogative of bestowing kingdoms and peerages on relatives and favor-ites. The political and economic power of the most lordly families grew through the first century AD and became dominant after Guangwu's thirty-two-year reign.

He and his immediate successors also made an effort to assist the farmers, who as always had suffered the most during the upheavals. The land tax was set at a low one-thirtieth of a family's harvest. A resettlement program offered rent-free state land to those who were willing to work it, and grants of grain — welfare payments, in effect — were given to the needy and to those victimized by such natural disasters as floods, earthquakes, and cattle epidemics.

Chinese imperialism revived toward the end of the first century, when an aggressive general named Ban Chao either conquered or intimidated into submission dozens of non-Chinese city-states along the trade routes in Xinjiang and central Asia. Ban, a fierce fighter who had earlier been miscast as an imperial librarian, became "protector general" of the western states and stretched China's influence to the eastern edge of Parthia's domain. After his death in AD 102, the empire again lost its ability to maintain itself in the West, and Chinese prestige began a century-long decline.

Eight of twelve sovereigns during the dynasty's second phase ascended to office before they were fifteen years of age. While the Han throne passed from one under-aged emperor to another, real power shifted among the imperial deputies and regents, consort families and, increasingly, the palace eunuchs. The chronic intrigues and machinations at court again gradually eroded the strength of the central government; provincial lords filled the vacuum. By the middle of the second century AD, the initial signs of decline — extravagance and decadence — were recognizable to perceptive observers. One of these was a scholar named Wang Fu.

Performers juggle balls, dance on drums, and execute handsprings on tables stacked twelve high in a variety show depicted in the bas-relief above. At right, an ebullient balladeer, with a broad smile on his face, beats a drum while he belts out his song. Musical storytelling was a popular form of entertainment during the Han dynasty, when it was common for musicians, dancers, and acrobats to enliven a banquet.

"Nowadays people are extravagant in clothing, excessive in food and drink, and fascinated with clever language," he wrote. "They become expert in the arts of deception. Some able-bodied men never learn how to handle plows and hoes, taking roaming and gambling as their profession. Moreover, many women do not cultivate cooking and have given up tending silkworms and weaving, instead taking up the study of shamanistic prayers, drumming, and dancing. At present the clothing, food and drink, carriages, adornment, and houses of the noble relatives in the capital all exceed even what is prescribed for kings. The rich compete to do better than one another while the poor are ashamed that they cannot keep up."

Eunuchs occupied a peculiar position in Han society. Their emasculation made them figures of contempt, but their proximity to the emperor gave them both privilege and political power. They rose to supreme authority after a confrontation in AD 168. That year, a regent who ruled in the name of Ling, a twelve-year-old Han emperor, decided to kill the eunuch leaders to assert his authority. But the troops he led to the palace deserted when the two sides faced off, and the regent killed himself.

Emperor Ling's subsequent twenty-one-year reign marked the apex of eunuch influence. Whereas in the dynasty's early years court eunuchs had numbered in the tens, their ranks now swelled to more than 2,000. During Ling's tenure, they killed scholar-officials who offended them and barred the relatives of these enemies from holding office. Unabashed in their corruption — perhaps because of their alienation from the old Han establishment and its ideals — the eunuchs brazenly put up for sale the highest positions in the empire. Five million of the standard coins, which apparently had no name other than "cash," bought one of the nine ministries. The going rate for the governorship of a commandery, apparently a more lucrative post, was twenty million coins.

The end of the eunuchs' heyday came soon afer Ling's death in 189. Two high-ranking army commanders petitioned the dowager for permission to execute all the court eunuchs. Learning of this plan, the eunuchs ambushed one of the officers and lopped off his head. The other commander assembled his troops and attacked the palace in force. This time the soldiers obeyed orders: They methodically slaughtered more than 2,000 eunuchs, leaving the imperial precincts awash in blood.

Military warlords now competed for control of the empire, and Ling's youthful successor became a hostage first to one general and then to another. The capital city of Luoyang was put to the torch in 190, its residents forced to take flight and trek overland through the lawless countryside to the former capital, Chang'an. The great empire of the Han deteriorated into anarchy: Armed bands roamed the land; the proud imperial officials were powerless. A poet captured the grim state of the realm in a vignette: "A starving woman beside the road / hugs her child, then lays it in the weeds, / looks back at the sound of its wailing, wipes her tears and goes on alone."

Three warlords — one in the north, one in the west, and the third in the south — eventually emerged as the chief contestants for the Han legacy. The leader in the north, Cao Cao, had possession of the puppet emperor and the remnants of his court. The end of the Han epoch, bloodless and timid as a soft sigh, came after Cao died in the year 220. The last emperor abdicated in favor of his protector's son. China drifted toward a reprise of the warring-states era.

The dust of fallen grandeur settled over Luoyang. "How still and desolate," a poet described it, "palaces and chambers all gutted and charred, every wall and fence row gaping and torn; thorns and brambles reach up to the sky."

	400 BC	350 BC	300 BC	250 BC	200 BC	150 BC
GREECE	Sparta dominates Greek city-states. Philip II becomes regent of Macedonia and expands the realm.	Philip becomes the ruler of Greece. Philip is assassinated. Alexander succeeds him and defeats the Persians in Asia Minor. Alexander campaigns into Egypt, where he is recognized as king. Alexander levels Persepolis. Darius is murdered by his own men. In India, Alexander's forced to turn back. Alexander dies in Babylon.	Pyrrhus of Epirus defeats the Romans encroaching on Greek colonies in southern Italy, but he sustains great losses and returns to Greece. Alexander's empire is divided into the kingdoms of Macedon, Seleucid, and Ptolemy.		Philip V of Macedon, after siding with Hannibal in the Punic Wars, is defeated by the Romans in the battle of Cynoscephalae in Thessaly and is driven back to Macedon.	Macedon becomes a Roman province. Slaves revolt in Attica, Sicily, Asia Minor, and Delos.
ROME	The Celts sack Rome but quickly withdraw.	Rome defeats and dissolves the Latin League.	With its victory over the Samnites, Rome achieves domination of central Italy. New legislation gives the plebeians a voice in the assembly. In the First Punic War with Carthage, Rome wins Sicily.	Rome is victorious in the Second Punic War against Hannibal. The Carthaginian's cunning campaign across the Alps won him many victories, but in the end Roman allies helped to turn the tide against him.	Rome defeats Antiochus of Syria at Magnesia and wins the western lands of Asia Minor for its allies Rhodes and Pergamum.	In the Third Punic War Rome levels Carthage, plows under the remains, and sows the furrows with salt. The Gracchi brothers introduce measures for land and social reforms. Rome conquers southern Gaul. Gaius Marius reforms the Roman military system.
INDIA AND PARTHIA		Chandragupta I unites northern India and establishes the Mauryan empire. Seleucus I founds the Seleucid dynasty to rule over most of the old Persian empire.	Mauryan king Asoka conquers Kalinga and assumes rule over most of India. Following his conquests, Asoka sends cultural missions to Syria, Egypt, Macedonia, Epirus, Burma, and Ceylon.	Arsaces I establishes the kingdom of Parthia between the Seleucid territory in the west and Bactria in the east.	The Sunga dynasty is founded in India and overthrows Mauryan rule. Mithradates I of Parthia wins Babylonia and Media from the Seleucids, then adds Elam and Persis to found the Parthian empire.	Phraates II of Parthia defeats the Seleucid king Antiochus VII in Media and thereby takes control of all lands east of the Euphrates. Mithradates II of Parthia defeats the Scythians and Armenians.
CHINA	Civil war continues among Chinese kingdoms, during what was later known as the Warring States Period.			The state of Qin conquers the last of its rivals under a ruler who calls himself Shi huangdi, meaning First Emperor. Shi huangdi orders the building of the Great Wall to keep out the Huns. Liu Bang conquers the lands of Qin and founds the Han dynasty.		Wu Di enlarges the Han empire by conquering southern China, northern Vietnam, northern Korea, and parts of central Asia.

Time Frame 400 BC-AD 200

100 BC	50 BC	0	AD 50	AD 100	AD 150	AD 200

Caesar's cohorts and successors carry out their internecine feuds on Greek soil in the battles of Pharsalus and Philippi.

Southern Epirus, the Ionian islands, and the Cyclades join with Greece to form the senatorial province of Achaea.

Western Asia Minor experiences a new flourishing of Greek culture.

A Greek era of prosperity begins under the Roman emperor Hadrian. Building resumes in Athens, and the city sprouts a suburb. The Panhellenic Games are instituted.

Roman civil war erupts.

Caesar proclaims himself dictator. One year later he is murdered.

The second triumvirate forms.

Mark Antony marries Cleopatra. Rome sends a fleet against Egypt and defeats Cleopatra's forces. Antony and Cleopatra commit suicide.

Octavian becomes emperor and calls himself Augustus.

The Thracian gladiator Spartacus leads a slave revolt in Rome.

Caesar, Pompey, and Crassus form the first triumvirate.

Caesar conquers much of Gaul.

Christ is born.

Augustus dies; his stepson Tiberius succeeds him.

Caligula succeeds Tiberius.

Claudius becomes emperor and conquers Britain.

Nero accedes to the throne.

Rome burns, giving Nero an excuse to begin the persecution of Christians.

Mount Vesuvius erupts and buries Pompeii and Herculaneum.

Under Trajan the empire reaches its greatest extent.

Hadrian suppresses the revolt of the Jews and denies them access to Jerusalem.

Marcus Aurelius, who would be called the last good emperor, rules for nineteen years, after which the empire begins its decline.

The Armenians recover and inflict great losses on the Parthians.

Phraates III restores order in Parthia but cannot withstand Roman advances.

The Parthian noble Suren defeats the Roman triumvir Crassus at Carrhae.

Phraates IV defeats Mark Antony's Roman army but loses Armenia.

The Kushan kingdom begins to thrive in northwest India.

Parthia falls apart into numerous small states and loses its importance.

Emperor Wang Mang undertakes radical social reforms.

Guang Wu Di restores Han rule and moves the court from Chang'an to Luoyang.

Buddhism is brought to China by missionaries from central Asia and India.

The Han Empire begins to fall apart, and in 220 the foundering empire is split up among three warlords.

ACKNOWLEDGMENTS

The editors wish to thank the following individuals and institutions for their valuable assistance with this volume:
England: Camberly, Surrey—John Warry, Political and Social Studies Department, Royal Military Academy, Sandhurst. London—Richard Blurton, Department of Oriental Antiquities, British Museum; Lucilla Burn, Department of Greek and Roman Antiquities, British Museum; Malcolm Colledge, Head of Department of Classics, Westfield College, University of London; Judith Swaddling, Department of Greek and Roman Antiquities; Brian A. Tremain, Photographic Service, British Museum; Vladimir Zwalf, Department of Oriental Antiquities, British Museum. Reading, Berkshire—J. G. Landels, Senior Lecturer in Classics, University of Reading. Spalding, Lincolnshire—Peter Connolly, Institute of Archaeology, University College.
France: Paris—Michel Amandry, Conservateur au Cabinet des Médailles; François Avril, Curateur, Département des Manuscrits, Bibliothèque Nationale; Christophe Barbotin, Conservateur du Département des Antiquités Egyptiennes, Musée du Louvre; Laure Beaumont-Maillet, Conservateur en Chef du Cabinet des Estampes, Bibliothèque Nationale; Catherine Bélanger, Chargée des Relations Extérieures du Musée du Louvre; Jeannette Chalufour, Archives Tallandier; Béatrice Coti, Directrice du Service Iconographique, Editions Mazenod; Antoinette Decaudin, Documentaliste, Département des Antiquités Orientales, Musée du Louvre; Thomas Drew-Bear, Directeur de Recherche, CNRS; Dominique Fayolle, Photothèque Musée Guimet; Michel Fleury, Président de la IVe Section de l'École Practique des Hautes Études; Marie-Françoise Huygues des Etages, Conservateur, Musée de la Marine; Françoise Jestaz, Conservateur du Cabinet des Estampes, Bibliothèque Nationale; Kate de Kersauson, Conservateur du Département des Antiquités Grecques et Romaines, Musée du Louvre; Joel Le Gall, Professeur Emérite à la Sorbonne Université; Marie Montembault, Documentaliste, Département des Antiquités Grecques et Romaines, Musée du Louvre; Marie-Odile Roy, Service Photographique, Bibliothèque Nationale; Jacqueline Sanson, Conservateur, Directeur du Service Photographique, Bibliothèque Nationale.
Germany (East Germany): Berlin—Volker Kästner, Antikensammlung Staatliche Museen zu Berlin.
Germany (West Germany): Berlin—Edmund Buchner, Präsident, Deutsches Archäologisches Institüt; Leonard Dolmans, Buchhandlung Wasmuth; Luca Juliani, Antikenmuseum Staatliche Museen Preussischer Kulturbesitz; Heidi Klein, Bildarchiv Preussischer Kulturbesitz; Gabrielle Kohler-Gallei, Archiv für Kunst und Geschichte; Gertrud Platz, Antikenmuseum Staatliche Museen Preussischer Kulturbesitz. Bonn—Dieter Salzmann, Archäologisches Institüt, Universität Bonn. Cologne—Hans Gerd Hellenkemper, Director, Römisch-Germanisches Museum; Friederike Naumann, Römisch-Germanisches Museum; Hansgeorg Stiegeler, Römisch-Germanisches Museum. Karlsruhe—Michael Maasz, Oberkonservator, Badisches Landesmuseum. Mainz—Karl-Viktor Decker, Oberkustos, Landesmuseum. Munich—Irmgard Ernstmeier, Hirmer Verlag; Friedrich Wilhelm Hamdorf, Oberkonservator, Staatliche Antikensammlungen und Glyptothek; Hirmer Verlag. Stockdorf—Claus Hansmann.
Trier— Hartwig Löhr, Rheinisches Landesmuseum.
Italy: Aquileia—Luisa Bertacchi, Director, Museo Archeologico. Naples—Enrica Pozzi, Superintendent, Soprintendenza Archeologico di Napoli; Valeria Sampaolo, Soprintendenza Archeologica di Napoli. Perugia—Filippo Coarelli, Dipartimento di Antichità Greche e Romane, University of Perugia. Pompeii—Baldassare Conticello, Superintendent, Soprintendenza Archeologica di Pompei; Antonio D'Ambrosio, Soprintendenza Archeologica di Pompei; Antonio Varrone, Soprintendenza Archeologica di Pompei. Rome—Maria Stella Arena, Superintendent, Soprintendenza Archeologica di Ostia; Maria Cataldi, Soprintendenza per le Antichità dell'Etruria Meridionale; Maria Rita di Mino, Soprintendenza Archeologica di Roma; Paola Germani, Soprintendenza Archeologica di Ostia; Carlo Ghislandi, Musei Vaticani; Adriano La Regina, Superintendent, Soprintendenza Archeologica di Roma; Maria Giuseppina Lauro, Soprintendenza Archeologica di Ostia; Anna Mura-Sommella, Director, Musei Capitolini; Paola Pelagatti, Superintendent, Soprintendenza per le Antichità dell'Etruria Meridionale; Maria Luisa Veloccia Rinaldi, Superintendent, Soprintendenza Archeologica per il Lazio.
Peoples' Republic of China: Beijing—Cultural Relics Publishing House, Chinese Archeological Overseas Exhibition Corporation. Kunming—Yunnan Provincial Museum.

The Chinese poems on pages **160** and **165** are reprinted from *Chinese Lyricism: Shih Poetry from the Second to the Twelfth Century*, translations by Burton Watson, © 1971, Columbia University Press, by permission of the publisher.

PICTURE CREDITS

BIBLIOGRAPHY

BOOKS

Amos, H. D., and A. G. P. Lang, *These Were the Greeks*. Chester Springs, Pa.: Dufour Editions, Inc.

Andronicos, Manolis, *Vergina: The Royal Tombs and the Ancient City*. Athens, Greece: Ekdotike Athenon S.A., 1984.

Baaren, Th. P. van, ed., et al., *Iconography of Religions*. Leiden, Holland: E. J. Brill, 1986.

Barrow, R. H., *The Romans*. Baltimore: Penguin Books, 1962.

Basham, A. L., *The Wonder That Was India*. New York: Hawthorn Books, Inc., 1963.

Boardman, John, Jasper Griffin, and Oswyn Murray, eds., *The Oxford History of the Classical World*. New York: Oxford University Press, 1986.

Bowra, C. M., *The Greek Experience*. Cleveland: World Publishing Co., 1957.

Brilliant, Richard, *Pompeii: AD 79*. New York: Clarkson N. Potter, 1979.

Brumbaugh, Robert S., *Ancient Greek Gadgets and Machines*. New York: Thomas Y. Crowell, 1966.

Brunt, P. A., *Social Conflicts in the Roman Republic*. New York: W. W. Norton & Co., 1971.

Caesar, Julius, *The Battle for Gaul*. Transl. by Anne Wiseman and Peter Wiseman. London: Chatto & Windus, 1980.

Carcopino, Jerome, *Daily Life in Ancient Rome*. Transl. by E. O. Larimer. New Haven: Yale University Press, 1940.

Casson, Lionel:
Ancient Trade and Society. Detroit: Wayne State University, 1984.
The Greek Conquerors. Chicago: Stonehenge Press, 1981.

Coarelli, Filippo, *Il Foro Romano*. Rome: Edizioni Quasar, 1983.

Colledge, Malcolm A. R.:
Parthian Art. Ithaca, New York: Cornell University Press, 1977.
The Parthian Period. Leiden, Holland: E. J. Brill, 1986.
The Parthians. New York: Frederick A. Praeger, 1967.

Connolly, Peter:
Hannibal and the Enemies of Rome. Morristown, N.J.: Silver Burdett, 1985.
Roman Army. Morristown, N.J.: Silver Burdett, 1978.

Cornell, Tim, and John Matthews, *Atlas of the Roman World*. New York: Facts on File Publications, 1986.

Cowell, F. R., *Everyday Life in Ancient Rome*. London: Batsford, 1961.

Crawford, Michael, *The Roman Republic*. Glasgow: William Collins Sons, 1978.

Debevoise, Neilson C., *A Political History of Parthia*. Chicago: University of Chicago Press, 1938.

De Camp, L. Sprague, *The Ancient Engineers*. Garden City, N.Y.: Doubleday, 1963.

De Fine Licht, Kjeld, *The Rotunda in Rome*. Copenhagen: Jutland Archaeological Society, 1966.

Dell'Orto, Luisa Franchi, *Ancient Rome: Life and Art*. Florence, Italy: Scala, 1982.

Dudley, Donald K., *Urbs Roma*. Oxford: Phaidon Press, 1967.

Errington, R. M., *The Dawn of Empire*. Ithaca, N.Y.: Cornell University Press, 1972.

Fox, Robin Lane, *The Search for Alexander*. London: Allen Lane, 1980.

Frontinus-Gesellschaft e. V., ed.:
Die Wasserversorgung Antiker Städte. Mainz, West Germany: Verlag Philip von Zabern, 1987.
Wasserversorgung im Antiken Rom. Munich: R. Oldenbourg Verlag, 1982.

Frye, Richard N., *The Heritage of Persia*. Cleveland: World Publishing Company, 1963.

Fustel de Coulanges, Numa Denis, *The Ancient City*. Garden City, N.Y.: Doubleday, 1956.

Gaitanides, Johannes, and Rudolf Schneider-Manns Au, *Traumfahrten durch die Ägäis*. Vienna: Verlag Fritz Molden, 1977.

Garzetti, Albino, *From Tiberius to the Antonines*. Transl. by J. R. Foster. London: Methuen & Co., 1974.

Grant, Michael:
The Art and Life of Pompeii and Herculaneum. New York: Newsweek and Arnoldo Mondadori Editore, 1979.
History of Rome. New York: Charles Scribner's Sons, 1979.
The Roman Forum. New York: Macmillan, 1970.
The World of Rome. New York: A Meridian Book, 1987.

Grant, Michael, ed., *Greece and Rome*. New York: Bonanza Books, 1986.

Greece and Rome: Builders of Our World. Washington, D.C.: National Geographic Society, 1968.

Hadas, Moses, and the Editors of Time-Life Books, *Imperial Rome* (Great Ages of Man series). Alexandria, Va.: Time-Life Books, 1979.

Hagen, Victor W. von:
The Roads That Led to Rome. London: George Weidenfeld and Nicholson Ltd., 1967.
Roman Roads. Cleveland: World Publishing Co., 1966.

Hamey, L. A., and J. A. Hamey, *The Roman Engineers*. Cambridge: Cambridge University Press, 1987.

Hamilton, Edith, *The Roman Way to Western Civilization*. New York: A Mentor Book, 1932.

Hammond, N. G. L., *A History of Greece to 322 B.C.* Oxford: Oxford University Press, 1984.

Hammond, N. G. L., and H. H. Scullard, eds., *The Oxford Classical Dictionary*. Oxford: Oxford University Press, 1978.

Harden, Donald B., *Glass of the Caesars*. Milan, Italy: Olivetti, 1987.

Heintze, Helga von, ed., *Römische Porträt-Plastik*. Stuttgart, West Germany: Hans E. Gunther Verlag, 1961.

Heinz, Werner, *Römische Thermen*. Munich: Hirmer Verlag, 1983.

Henig, Martin, ed., *A Handbook of Roman Art*. Oxford: Phaidon, 1983.

Hibbert, Christopher, *The Emperors of China* (Treasures of the World series). Chicago: Stonehenge Press, 1981.

Hicks, Jim, and the Editors of Time-Life Books, *The Persians* (The Emergence of Man series). New York: Time-Life Books, 1975.

Holland, Jack, and John Monroe, *The Order of Rome.* New York: HBJ Press, 1980.

Honle, Augusta, and Anton Henze, *Römische Amphitheater und Stadien.* Zurich, Switzerland: Atlantis, 1981.

Huart, Clement, *Ancient Persia and Iranian Civilization.* New York: Barnes & Noble, 1972.

Jenkins, Ian, *Greek and Roman Life.* Cambridge, Mass.: Harvard University Press, 1986.

Jones, A. H. M., *Augustus.* New York: W. W. Norton & Co., 1970.

Kitto, H. D. F., *The Greeks.* Chicago: Aldine Publishing Co., 1964.

Lamprecht, Heinz-Otto, *Opus Caementitium.* Düsseldorf, West Germany: Beton-Verlag, 1985.

La Rocca, Eugenio, *Ara Pacis Augustae.* Rome: L'Erma di Bretschneider, 1983.

La Rocca, Eugenio, Mariette de Vos, and Arnold de Vos, *Guida Archeologica di Pompei.* Milan: Arnoldo Montadori Editore, 1976.

Latourette, Kenneth Scott, *The Chinese: Their History and Culture.* New York: Macmillan, 1964.

Lissner, Ivar, *The Caesars: Might and Madness.* Transl. by J. Maxwell Brownjohn. New York: G. P. Putnam's Sons, 1958.

Loewe, Michael, *Everyday Life in Early Imperial China.* London: Carousel Books, 1973.

McCrindle, J. W., *Ancient India as Described by Megasthenes and Arrian.* Calcutta: Chuckervertty, Chatterjee & Co., 1926.

MacDonald, William L., *The Architecture of the Roman Empire:*
Vol. 1, *An Introductory Study.* New Haven: Yale University Press, 1982.
Vol. 2, *An Urban Appraisal,* New Haven: Yale University Press, 1986.

MacKendrick, Paul, *Roman France.* New York: St. Martin's Press, 1972.

Majumdar, R. C., *Ancient India.* Delhi: Motilal Banarsidass, 1977.

Mossé, Claude, ed., *Athens in Decline 404-86 B.C.* Transl. by Jean Stewart. London: Routledge & Kegan Paul, 1973.

Nash, Ernest, *Pictorial Dictionary of Ancient Rome.* Vol. 1. New York: Frederick A. Praeger, 1961.

The New Illustrated Columbia Encyclopedia. New York: Columbia University Press, 1979.

Ogden, Jack, *Jewellery of the Ancient World.* New York: Rizzoli, 1982.

Pirazzoli-t'Serstevens, Michèle, *The Han Dynasty.* Transl. by Janet Seligman. New York: Rizzoli, 1982.

Plommer, Hugh, *Vitruvius and Later Roman Building Manuals.* Cambridge: Cambridge University Press, 1973.

Plutarch:
The Age of Alexander. Transl. by Ian Scott-Kilvert. Harmondsworth, Middlesex, England: Penguin Books, 1985.
The Lives of the Noble Grecians. Transl. by John Dryden. New York: The Modern Library, no date.

Potter, T. W., *Roman Britain.* London: British Museum Publications, 1984.

Renault, Mary, *The Nature of Alexander.* New York: Pantheon Books, 1975.

Sakellariou, M. B., ed., *Macedonia: 4000 Years of Greek History and Civilization.* Athens: Ekdotike Athenon S.A., 1983.

Salmon, E. T., *The Making of Roman Italy.* Ithaca, N.Y.: Cornell University Press, 1982.

Schafer, Edward H., and the Editors of Time-Life Books, *Ancient China* (Great Ages of Man series). New York: Time-Life Books, 1976.

Schulberg, Lucille, and the Editors of Time-Life Books, *Historic India* (Great Ages of Man series). Alexandria, Va.: Time-Life Books, 1979.

Schwartzberg, Joseph E., ed., *A Historical Atlas of South Asia.* Chicago: University of Chicago Press, 1978.

Sear, Frank, *Roman Architecture.* Ithaca, N.Y.: Cornell University Press, 1983.

Sherratt, Andrew, ed., *The Cambridge Encyclopedia of Archaeology.* Scarborough, Ontario: Prentice-Hall of Canada / Cambridge University Press, 1980.

Simon, Erika, *Augustus.* Munich: Hirmer Verlag, 1986.

Sitwell, N. H. H., *Roman Roads of Europe.* London: Cassell, 1981.

Stead, I. M., *Celtic Art in Britian before the Roman Conquest.* London: British Museum Publications, 1985.

Strong, Donald, *Roman Art.* Harmondsworth, Middlesex, England: Penguin Books, 1980.

Suetonius, *The Twelve Caesars.* Transl. by Robert Graves. Harmondsworth, Middlesex, England: Penguin Books, 1987.

Tarn, W. W., and G. T. Griffith, *Hellenistic Civilisation.* London: Edward Arnold, 1952.

Taylor, Lily Ross, *Party Politics in the Age of Caesar.* Berkeley: University of California Press, 1949.

Temple, Robert K. G., *China: Land of Discovery.* Wellingborough, Northhamptonshire, England: Patrick Stevens, 1986.

Thapar, Romila:
Aśoka and the Decline of the Mauryas. Oxford: Oxford University Press, 1961.
A History of India. Vol. 1. Harmondsworth, Middlesex, England: Penguin Books, 1984.

T'ung-tsu Ch'ü, *Han Social Structure.* Seattle: University of Washington Press, 1972.

Twitchett, Denis, and Michael Loewe, eds., *The Ch'in and Han Empires, 221 B.C.-A.D. 220.* Vol. 1 of *The Cambridge History of China.* Cambridge: Cambridge University Press, 1986.

Wang Zhongshu, *Han Civilization.* Transl. by K. C. Chang et al. New Haven: Yale University Press, 1982.

Ward-Perkins, J. B., *Roman Imperial Architecture.* Harmondsworth, Middlesex, England: Penguin Books, 1985.

Watson, Burton, *Chinese Lyricism: Shih Poetry from the Second to the Twelfth Century.* New York: Columbia University Press, 1971.

Watson, Francis, *A Concise History of India.* New York: Charles Scribner's Sons, 1975.

Webster, T. B. L., *The Age of Greece: The Age of Hellenism.* New York: Crown Publishers, 1966.

Webster's Biographical Dictionary. Springfield, Mass.: G. & C. Merriam, 1976.

Werner, Dietrich, *Wasser für das Antike Rom.* Berlin: VEB Verlag für Bauwesen, 1986.

Wilbur, C. Martin, *Slavery in China during the Former Han Dynasty.* New York: Russell & Russell, 1967.

Wilcken, Ulrich, *Alexander the Great.* Transl. by G. C. Richards. New York: W. W. Norton, 1967.

Wolpert, Stanley, *A New History of India.* New York: Oxford University Press, 1982.

Yarshater, Ehsan, ed., *The Seleucid, Parthian and Sasanian Periods.* Vol. 3 (2) of *The Cambridge History of Iran.* Cambridge: Cambridge University Press, 1983.

OTHER SOURCES

Bothmer, Dietrich von, *A Greek and Roman Treasury.* The Metropolitan Museum of Art, 1984.

Museo dell Civiltà Romana, *Il Trionfo dell'Acqua.* Rome: Paleani Editrice, 1986.

Topping, Audrey, "China's Incredible Find." *National Geographic,* April 1978.

Ward-Perkins, John, and Amanda Claridge, *Pompeii: AD 79.* New York: Alfred Knopf and the Museum of Fine Arts, Boston, 1978.

INDEX

culties, 62-63, 88; emblems of, *42-43;* emperors, 76-78, *79-82,* 83-88; empire of, 36, *map* 46, 50, 52-55, 58-62, 76, 86-88, 123-126; gladiatorial games, 45, 47, *64-65,* 70, 76; life in, 45-50, *54,* 66; merchant class, 62, 63; obelisk sundial, *77;* opulence of, 45, 127, *128-137;* and Parthians, 114, 123-126; plague in, 88, 126; Republic ends, 75-76; roads, 89, *94-95;* slavery, 47, 59, 63, 71; social conflict in, 50-51, 66, 69, 75. *See also:* Art; Government; Law; Religion; *names of individual deities and rulers*
Romulus (Roman hero), 45
Roxane (Alexander's wife), 29, 35
Rubicon River, 73

S

Sacae (Asian nomads), 115-118
Sacred Band, 12, 16, 18, 19
Saguntum (Spanish city), 56
Samarkand (Asian city), 29, 149
Sanchi, Buddhist shrine at, *112-113*
Sardinia, 55
Sardis (Greek city), 24
Sassanians, 37, 40
Satala (Asian city), sculpture from, *120*
Science: China, 139, 152, *160,* 161; Greece, 160, *161-162;* Ptolemaic Egypt, 35
Scipio Aemililianus, Publius Cornelius (Roman consul), 58
Scipio Africanus, Publius Cornelius, 58, 62
Scipio Asiaticus, Lucius Cornelius, 62
Scopas (Greek artist), 13
Scythians, 114
Sejanus (Roman politician), 83
Seleucia (Syrian city), 119, 123, 126
Seleucids, 35, 36, 62, 101, 102, 111-115, 123
Seleucus I Nicator (Seleucid ruler), 36, 106, 111
Senate, Roman, 50, 51, 66, 67, 69, 71-73, 75, 78, 83, 84, 86
Shang dynasty, 141
Shelley, Percy Bysshe, quoted, 93
Shi Huangdi (Chinese emperor), 140-146, 154; tomb of, 143, *144-145*
Ships, Roman, 55
Sicily, 55, 58

Siddhartha Gautama, 106. *See also* Buddha
Silk, *151,* 156; trade in, *map* 116-117, 149
Silk Road, *116-117,* 118, 126, 149, 163
Sin (Parthian deity), *115*
Slavery, 47, 59, 63, 71, 158, 162
Smallpox, 126
Social War, 67-69
Socrates (Greek philosopher), 15; quoted, 13
Sogdiana, 29
Spain, 55, 58, 70
Sparta (Greek city), 11-12
Spartacus (rebel slave), 71
Strabo (Greek historian), 89
Struggle of the Orders, 51
Suetonius (Roman historian), quoted, 79, 81, 82, 84
Sulla, Lucius Cornelius (Roman general), 67-70, 123
Suren (Parthian nobleman), 123, 125
Susa (Persian city), 27, 31
Syria, 62, 70, 109, 114

T

Tacitus (Roman historian), 114; quoted, 84, 85
Tarentum (Greek colony), 53
Tashkent (Asian city), 149
Technology: Chinese, 139, *151-155,* 156-158, *160,* 161; Indian, 105; Roman, 89, *162. See also* Engineering
Terence (Roman dramatist), 78
Thebes (Greek city), 12, 16, 18, 19, 23
Thermopylae, second battle of, 62
Thessaly, 16, 18
Thrace, 16, 22
Tiberius (Roman emperor), 78, 81, 83, 136
Tibet, *map* 140
Tigris River, 111, 114, 126
Titus (Roman emperor), 82, 86, 91
Tou Wan (Chinese princess), jade burial suit of, *148-149*

Trade: Alexandria and Hellenistic world, 35; China, 149-150; India, 103, 105, 109; Parthia, 103, 116, 118; Rome, 47. *See also* Silk Road
Trajan (Roman emperor), 45, 65, *82,* 86-88
Transalpine Gaul, 71
Triumvirate (Roman): First, 71; Second, 75
Troy, 24
Turkestan, 29
Tyre (Phoenician city), 26

U

Uxellodunum (Celtic hill fort), 72

V

Venus (Roman deity), 76, 93
Vercingetorix (Celtic chieftain), 70
Verethraghna (Parthian deity), 119
Vespasian (Roman emperor), 49, 79, *82,* 86
Vesuvius, Mount, eruption of, 59, 63
Vietnam. *See* Annam
Virgil (Roman poet), 78

W

Wang Fu (Chinese scholar), 165
Wang Mang (Chinese emperor), 162
Warfare: Actium, battle of, 75; Cannae, battle of, 57; Carrhae, battle of, 123-125; Chaeronea, battle of, 19; Chinese warriors, *143-145,* 147-148; Gallic campaigns, *70,* 71-72; Gaugamela, battle of, *map* 10-11, 27; Granicus, battle of, *map* 10-11, 24; Hydaspes, battle of, 30; Indian bow, 103; Indian war elephants, *104-105;* Issus, battle of, *map* 22, *22-23,* 24; Italian wars, 52-53; Macedonian army, 16-18; Macedonian wars, 58-62; Magnesia ad Sipylum, battle of, 62; Masada, siege of, 86; naval, 55, 75; Parthian cavalry, 122-123, *124-125,* 126; Philippi, battle of, 75; Phrygian helmet, *20;* Punic wars, 50, 55-58, 62; Roman soldiers, 51, 62, 67, *68;* Roman trophies, *136, 137;* Social War, 67-69; Theban infantry, 12, 18; Thermopylae, second battle of, 62; Warring States Period, 139-140; Zama, battle of, 58

Warring States Period, 139-140
Wei (Chinese kingdom), 140
Wei River, 139, 146
Wen (Chinese emperor), 147, 156
Women: in Chinese society, 147, 155, 159, 162; in Greek society, 27; in Indian society, 107, 109; in Parthian society, 118
Writing: Chinese characters standardized, 141; cuneiform, 36
Wu Di (Chinese emperor), 147, 148, 150-152, 155, 161

X

Xenophon (Greek historian), 13, 22
Xian. *See* Chang'an
Xiang Yu (Chinese general), 146
Xianyang (Chinese city), 141
Xin dynasty, 162
Xingjiang, 163
Xiongnu (Asian tribe), 142, 147-149, 163

Y

Yan (Chinese kingdom), 140
Yellow River, flooding of, 163
Yueh (Asian tribe), 142
Yuezhi (Asian tribe), 148-149

Z

Zama, battle of, 58
Zeus (Greek deity), 24, 26, 31, 42, 119
Zeus-Amon (Hellenic deity), *120*
Zeus-Oramsdes (Hellenic deity), 119
Zhang Meng (Chinese inventor), 161
Zhang Qian (Chinese explorer), 148-149, 150
Zhao (Chinese kingdom), 140
Zhao Gao, 146
Zhou dynasty, 139, 141, 142, 163
Zoroaster, 122
Zoroastrianism, 122